Morton Rhue

Asphalt Tribe

Morton Rhue wurde 1950 in New York City geboren. Der mehrfach preisgekrönte Autor einer Vielzahl von Romanen für Jugendliche ist in Deutschland vor allem durch »Die Welle« bekannt geworden. Nach seinem Literaturstudium verdiente er seinen Lebensunterhalt teilweise als Straßenmusiker in Europa, später arbeitete er vornehmlich als Journalist. Heute widmet er sich fast ausschließlich seiner schriftstellerischen Tätigkeit neben Lesungen und Workshops in Schulen.

Von Morton Rhue sind in den Ravensburger Taschenbüchern erschienen:

RTB 58008
Die Welle

RTB 58172
Ich knall euch ab!

RTB 58212
Asphalt Tribe

RTB 58213
Asphalt Tribe (englische Ausgabe)

RTB 58255
Boot Camp

RTB 58256
Boot Camp (englische Ausgabe)

RTB 58355
Ghetto Kidz

RTB 58356
Ghetto Kidz (englische Ausgabe)

RTB 58377
Fame Junkies

RTB 58381
Die Welle – Eine Graphic Novel

RTB 58452
Über uns Stille

Morton Rhue

ASPHALT TRIBE

Ravensburger Buchverlag

Als Ravensburger Taschenbuch
Band 58213
erschienen 2005

Glossar: Thorsten Dittmann
Umschlagillustration: Dirk Lieb
unter Verwendung von Fotos
von Sibylle Krebs
Lektorat: Petra Deistler

Printed in Germany

8 9 10 16 15 14

ISBN 978-3-473-58213-6

www.ravensburger.de

Preface

Each year in the United States 2.8 million teens run away from home. Most of these young people return home within 24–72 hours. But many stay away much longer. Sometimes for weeks and even months. Sometimes for years. And some never return home.

Today there are nearly 300,000 permanently homeless teenagers in the United States.
Why do so many children leave home? Most leave because of emotional, physical and/or sexual abuse. Among the general population roughly 2 % of all teenagers have experienced sexual abuse at home. But among homeless teens it is nearly 40 %.

My interest in writing about homeless teens began accidentally one day three years ago after speaking at a conference in Denver, Colorado. On the way back to the airport my

17 **abuse:** Missbrauch. **general population:** allgemeine Bevölkerung.
22 **accidentally** (adv.): zufällig.

host asked if I would mind stopping at a shelter for homeless teens while she dropped off some leftover food. It was a cold gray day, and a group of homeless kids were sitting around the shelter's only television. Even though they were in a shelter that had showers and laundry facilities for them, the room smelled of body odor and their clothes were stained and filthy. I was instantly curious. Did they not care about how they looked and smelled? Did this somehow mean they'd given up hope of going back to what we consider "normal" society? Or was it a deliberate statement? The uniform these "outsiders" wore. I managed to speak briefly to the kids and then got a tour of the shelter.

Back in New York I began to do research. I learned that there were different kinds of street kids with different kinds of attitudes. Some truly have given up on life and go through each day without purpose or reason. Others wear the dirt and odor of homelessness like a badge of their outsider status.

Soon I was on the Internet to get an idea of the numbers involved. I also learned that there was yet another type of homeless youth that I had never known about. These were

1 **shelter for homeless teens:** Heim für obdachlose Jugendliche. 2 **to drop off:** abliefern. 5 **laundry facilities:** Waschmaschinen. 6 **odor:** Geruch; Gestank. 7 **instantly:** sofort, augenblicklich. 10 **deliberate:** absichtlich; bewusst. **statement:** Aussage, Stellungnahme. 14 **to do research:** recherchieren. 18 **badge:** Abzeichen.

the homeless "club" kids who spend their days sleeping and their nights in dance clubs.

They are not easy to track down, as you only find them late outside clubs in NYC. A lot of them don't start partying until midnight. It was easier to find homeless street kids to speak to in the East Village. In New York City alone there are between 12,000 and 20,000 homeless youth. Nearly two-thirds are black or Latino. A large number of them are gay, lesbian, bisexual, or transgender. 47 % of homeless teens are homeless because they have been thrown out of their homes. Many of them have been thrown out of their homes because of their sexuality.

Because they have no way of earning money, many homeless teenagers engage in what is called survival sex. That is, they perform sexual acts in return for money, or a place to stay for the night, or food, or drugs, or even clothing. Remarkably, most street kids know about Aids and understand that by engaging in prostitution they run the risk of catching that deadly disease. But because they feel helpless and powerless they do little or nothing to avoid it. In fact, there is a high expectation among street kids that they will contract Aids. Homeless teens are ten times more likely to have Aids than

3 **to track down:** aufspüren. 8 **gay:** schwul. 9 **transgender:** Transgender-Persönlichkeit (Mensch, der sich nicht eindeutig einem Geschlecht zugehörig fühlt). 15 **to engage in:** sich beteiligen an. **survival:** Überleben. 16 **to perform sexual acts:** sexuelle Handlungen praktizieren. **in return for:** als Gegenleistung für. 23 **to be ten times more likely to have Aids:** mit einer zehnfach höheren Wahrscheinlichkeit Aids haben.

teens living with their families. And they are even more likely to have other sexually transmitted diseases. 94% of all homeless children ages 12 and up have been sexually active. 34% of all homeless females become pregnant. Among homeless females age 13 to 15, the rate of pregnancy is 14 times higher than girls that age who live at home.

As you no doubt know, a very high percentage of street kids use drugs and/or alcohol. They take more drugs and drink more alcohol because their pain and suffering is greater than that of teenagers who feel loved and secure in their homes. Less than ten per cent of teenagers living at home ever try hard drugs like heroin and crack cocaine. But nearly half of all homeless teenagers have tried these drugs. 25 % – that is, one quarter of all homeless teens – have attempted suicide. Every year in the United States, more than 5,000 homeless teens die on the streets. Roughly 14 teens a day. Most are buried in unmarked graves.

There are many different kinds of homeless kids. Some stay in one city. Others roam constantly from place to place. Some are filthy and smelly. Others hang around clubs and manage through prostitution and other means to have very

11 **secure:** sicher. 15 **to attempt suicide:** einen Selbstmordversuch unternehmen. 18 **unmarked grave:** anonymes Grab. 21 **to roam:** streunen. 22 **filthy:** dreckig. **to hang around clubs:** sich in Clubs herumtreiben.

fashionable clothes. But almost all homeless children have one thing in common: They feel abandoned by their families, unwanted and unloved.

Morton Rhue

1 **to have one thing in common:** eine Sache gemeinsam haben. 2 **to abandon:** aussetzen; aufgeben.

“Here is where you are.
There is where you want to be.
But you can’t get there from here.”

Harrison Blanchard aka OG

ONE

New Year's Eve

Maggot said we should go up to Times Square to watch the ball drop and pick some pockets, but we never got around to it. Instead we hung out in front of the *Good Life Deli* like we always did. Maggot, Rainbow, 2Moro, and me. A cold mist drifted out of the dark, the little droplets sparkling in the streetlights. Maggot and me sat under the awning of the newspaper stand on the corner. The damp matted down our hair. Black puddles dotted the street and steam rose like ghosts from the manhole covers. Rainbow sat cross-legged against the wall, loose strands of blond hair falling out of a blue wool cap, her head nodding almost down to her lap. 2Moro leaned against the streetlight with her arms crossed, not saying anything to anyone, just waiting for someone to say something to her.

It was one of those nights when there wasn't much traffic on the streets of New York. Most of the New Year's partiers

8 **to watch the ball drop:** Am Times Square verfolgen die New Yorker traditionell den Abstieg einer erleuchteten Kugel vom Fahnenmast eines Hochhauses, der den Beginn des neuen Jahres anzeigt. 9 **to pick some pockets:** ein paar Leute beklauen. **to get around to s.th.:** zu etwas kommen. 12 **mist:** Nebel. **droplet:** Tröpfchen. 13 **awning:** Vordach. 16 **manhole cover:** Gullideckel.

were done with their stupid celebrations and back in the four-walled cells they called apartments. Prisoners of the system, Maggot said. Now, only the newspaper delivery trucks and taxis passed, their tires making squishy noises on the wet, black pavement. Out here in the cold where we weren't walled in, we were free to go where we pleased.

"Guess the cops have the night off," Maggot said, his brown dreadlocks stringy from the mist; his breath a small cloud of fog.

"The rest of the world, too," muttered 2Moro. She was wearing a red-and-orange patchwork jacket, a tight black skirt, and high black boots. Her short dyed red hair was matted down on her forehead like a cap. Her piercings glinted in the streetlight. Tattooed around her neck was a circle of black barbed wire.

I sipped cold coffee from a paper cup. At night we drank coffee to stay awake. It was safer to sleep during the day.

A man and a woman came around the corner wearing raincoats and sharing a red umbrella. They slowed down when they saw us. The woman slid her arm through the man's and said something in his ear. Probably wanted him to turn around and go another way. But the man shook his head. Taking stiff strides, they walked toward us through the mist.

1 **to be done with s.th.:** mit etwas fertig sein. 4 **squishy:** matschig; zischend. 6 **to be walled in:** von Mauern umgeben sein. 7 **cop:** Bulle. **to have the night off:** die Nacht über frei haben, keinen Dienst haben. 8 **stringy:** faserig; lang und dünn. 13 **to be matted down:** wie angeklatscht sein. 15 **barbed wire:** Stacheldraht. 23 **to take stiff strides:** steifen Schrittes gehen.

When they got near, the woman wrinkled her nose like something smelled bad.

"Have fun tonight?" Maggot asked, kind of menacing.

The couple broke stride. "Yes, we did," the man answered.

"No work tomorrow, huh?" Maggot said. "Get to sleep in."

"That's right."

"Day after that it's back to the old nine-to-five grind," Maggot said.

"You could say that," answered the man.

"Happy New Year," said 2Moro, not in a friendly way.

"Same to you," said the man. He and the woman hurried past. She kept glancing over her shoulder at us until they reached the next corner.

"Robots," Maggot said. "Just following the rules. Work till they die. Then new robots replace them."

"Check this." 2Moro tilted her head down the sidewalk. A man was coming toward us, unsteady, dragging the toes of his shoes. The shoulders of his suit were dark with water and his white shirt collar was open, a blue-and-red tie hanging like an upside-down noose. His face was clean-shaven and his wet hair fell flat on his forehead.

We watched as he stumbled along, not yet aware of us. When he passed under a streetlight, something gold glinted

3 **menacing:** bedrohlich. 4 **to break stride:** stehen bleiben. 7 **grind:** Schufterei. 11 **to hurry past:** vorbeieilen. 12 **to glance at s.o.:** jdm. einen Blick zuwerfen. 16 **sidewalk:** Bürgersteig. 18 **suit:** Anzug. 19 **tie:** Schlips, Krawatte. 20 **noose:** Schlinge. 22 **to stumble:** stolpern.

on his wrist and light reflected off his wet polished leather shoes.

"Come to daddy," Maggot whispered, cracking his knuckles.

From her seat against the wall Rainbow raised her head. "Oh, Maggot, you're so full of it. You never rolled a drunk in your life."

"People do it all the time. How hard could it be?"

"He's big," I said.

"Bigger they are, the harder they fall." Maggot rose to his feet. "He'll never know what hit him."

"Let's do it," said 2Moro. She crossed the sidewalk and joined Maggot in the shadow of the newsstand awning.

Rainbow pressed her hands against the ground and tried to push herself up. "Come on, Maybe. Time to get outta here." But she lost her grip and slid back down.

"Try again." I put my hands under the arms of her leather jacket and helped her up. Out of the corner of my eye I saw the drunk guy a dozen yards away down the dark, wet sidewalk. He looked up, saw us, and stopped. I got Rainbow to her feet, turned her by the shoulders, and started to lead her away.

We were halfway down the block when the scuffle began.

3 **to crack one's knuckles:** mit den Fingerknöckeln knacken. 6 **to roll a drunk:** einen Betrunkenen ausnehmen. 16 **to lose one's grip:** den Halt verlieren. 19 **yard:** Yard (Längenmaß, 91 cm). 23 **scuffle:** Rauferei, Handgemenge.

Maggot and 2Moro trying to wrestle the drunk down. Maggot pulling at the guy's jacket from the front. 2Moro hitting him from behind. Only the drunk didn't seem to get the idea. 2Moro and Maggot hardly came up to his shoulders. He swung his arms and Maggot went down. Then he grabbed 2Moro and threw her so hard she disappeared between two parked cars. The drunk took a step, tripped over Maggot and fell to his hands and knees. Maggot got up and jumped on his back. 2Moro came out from between the parked cars and started to kick the guy in the sides.

The guy yanked Maggot down to the sidewalk and straddled him. 2Moro was still kicking and hitting him, but the guy hardly seemed to notice. Pinned on his back, Maggot flailed with open hands. The drunk slammed his fist into Maggot's face. Down the block Rainbow and me heard the crunching sound and saw Maggot go limp on the sidewalk. The drunk grabbed 2Moro by the wrist. She tried to shake free, but he wouldn't let go. He staggered to his feet and pulled his fist back like he was going to hit her next.

"Hey, don't!" I yelled and ran back toward them. I hated it when kids got hit. Got hit too many times myself. Not just with fists, neither.

1 **to wrestle:** ringen. 11 **to yank:** reißen. **to straddle:** rittlings sitzen auf. 13 **pinned:** gepresst. 14 **to flail:** wild um sich schlagen. 16 **crunching:** knirschend; knackend. 18 **to stagger to one's feet:** schwankend auf die Beine kommen.

Still holding 2Moro by the wrist, the drunk turned. I stopped a dozen feet away. “Please don’t hurt her, Mister. Please?”

The guy stared at me. “They jumped me,” he yelled.

“They’re just kids. They didn’t mean it.”

“Didn’t mean it? You crazy? They were kickin’ and hittin’ me. They wanted to rob me.”

Maggot sat up on the sidewalk, hands covering his mouth and nose, dark red blood seeping out between his fingers. The drunk still had 2Moro by the wrist. She kept swinging, trying to hit him.

“Let me go!” she screeched.

“Let her go,” I said. “She’s just a girl. Please?”

“You kiddin’ me? She’s twice as bad as him.” He pointed at Maggot.

“Just let her go,” I said. “I promise she won’t hurt you.”

“I’m gonna kill this pig!” 2Moro screamed, still clawing and scraping like a wild animal. The guy twisted her arm tighter.

“Ow!” 2Moro yelped.

“You better stop,” I told her, “or he’s gonna hurt you bad.”

2Moro stopped.

“If I let go, you gonna go quietly?” the drunk asked.

“Drop dead,” 2Moro spit.

2 **foot** (*pl.* feet): Fuß (Längenmaß, 30 cm). 4 **they didn’t mean it:** sie haben es nicht so gemeint. 8 **to seep out:** hindurchsickern. 9 **wrist:** Handgelenk. 16 **to claw:** kratzen. 17 **to scrape:** kratzen; abschürfen. **to twist:** verdrehen. 19 **to yelp:** jaulen. 23 **Drop dead!:** Geh zum Teufel!

He yanked her arm up behind her back. 2Moro let out a squeal and went limp. "Okay, okay," she whimpered. The man let go and 2Moro stumbled away, cradling her wrist. The whole thing must have sobered the guy up, because he stood straighter and tightened the blue-and-red tie around his collar. He looked down at his suit. The knee was torn. "Look what you kids did."

"Sorry," I said.

"Sorry?" he repeated. "Your friends jump me and you're sorry?"

"They just wanted some money."

"Then they should've asked." He looked around. Maggot was sitting on the sidewalk, staring at the blood on his hands. Down the block Rainbow was leaning against another wall, her head and shoulders again dipping toward her waist, 2Moro had sat down next to her.

"Just a bunch of homeless punks out to roll some drunks on New Year's Eve," the guy grumbled in disgust.

"No kidding," Maggot muttered.

"Well, you picked the wrong drunk." The guy started to walk away. Then he reached into his pocket and tossed out a handful of loose change. As the coins clattered onto the sidewalk, he said, "Happy New Year."

2 **squeal:** Kreischen; Aufschrei. **limp:** schlaff, schlapp. 3 **to cradle one's wrist:** sich das Handgelenk halten. 6 **collar:** Kragen. 18 **in disgust:** angeekelt, angewidert. 21 **to toss out:** wegwerfen. 22 **loose change:** Wechselgeld.

TWO

Alexander Mittelson, aka Country Club. *Born in Shaker Heights, Ohio. Father, a lawyer, and mother, a law professor at Case Western Law School. Divorced when Alexander was five. Two sisters, one married and living in Cleveland, the other in Los Angeles. Age 8, Alexander was diagnosed with Attention Deficit Hyperactivity Disorder. School performance dropped despite medication and extra academic support. Age 14, diagnosis of depression added. Often irritable, emotionally labile, and co-morbid. Frequent school tardiness and absences. Self-medication using drugs and alcohol. Age 16, stopped attending school. Age 17, ran away from home. Itinerant derelict. Frequent arrests for, loitering, petty larceny, public intoxication. Last known address, New York City. Dead at the age of 22. Cause of death: liver failure due to chronic alcohol poisoning.*

8 **aka:** (Abk. für *also known as*) alias. 13 **Attention Deficit Hyperactivity Disorder:** Hyperaktivitätsstörung. 17 **co-morbid:** unter psychischen Zusatzerkrankungen leidend (z.B. Borderline-Störung). 20 **itinerant derelict:** umherziehender Obdachloser. 21 **loitering:** unberechtigter Aufenthalt. **petty larceny:** Kleindiebstahl. **public intoxication:** Trunkenheit in der Öffentlichkeit.

Country Club was lying in Piss Alley next to a Christmas tree someone had thrown out of a window. The Christmas tree was on its side; Country Club lay on his back. His eyes were open. Glassy and dull. Like he was staring straight up at heaven. Sometimes on sunny days Country Club's eyes looked green. But on this cold gloomy day his eyes were as gray as the clouds overhead.

Under a film of dirt Country Club's skin was pasty and almost green. He had a wispy light brown beard, thin so you could see through it to his jaw and chin. On his left cheekbone was a long, crusty brown scab. On his right cheek was a small black tattoo of a spider's web. His long, tangled hair was spread out on the ground, mixed in with the torn papers and candy wrappers and bent straws that littered the alley. Bits of paper and dirt and a single strand of silver Christmas tinsel clung to his beard. His arms were spread out. One hand turned up, the other turned down. His hips were twisted sideways, his legs bent at the knees like he was running.

But he wasn't going nowhere.

Piss Alley smelled like pee because the restaurants and stores wouldn't let us use their bathrooms. OG was on his knees beside Country Club, sobbing. The tears left light trails

1 **alley:** Gasse, Weg. 4 **dull:** trüb. 8 **pasty:** blässlich. 9 **wispy:** dünn. 11 **scab:** Schorf. 12 **tangled:** verheddert. 14 **candy wrapper:** Verpackung einer Süßigkeit. 15 **Christmas tinsel:** Weihnachtsschmuck. 23 **to sob:** (laut) schluchzen. **trail:** Spur.

down his filthy cheeks. When street people cried, their tears were filmy with grime.

OG's hair was long and dirty blond, dreadlocked, and he had a bushy blond beard. One of his earlobes was stretched to the size of a silver dollar and had a clear round plastic plug in it. He wore bars and rings in his eyebrows, nose, and lips. OG and Country Club were partners. They traveled all over together.

OG let out a gurgly, liquid cough. He put his hands on the ground to brace himself, then coughed and coughed while his thin body shook. Then spit out a mouthful of greenish phlegm.

Maggot, Tears, and me stood nearby, watching. My stomach growled and hurt from hunger.

"He must've died during the night," Maggot said. His nose and the left side of his mouth were swollen purple and blue where the drunk guy punched him. His sweatshirt had a big reddish brown dried bloodstain on the front.

"How?" Tears asked. The newest and youngest member of our "family," she showed up a couple of weeks ago.

"Don't know," Maggot said. "Doesn't look like he was killed. I don't see any blood or bruises."

Maggot talked different from the rest of us. We would have said, "don't see no bruises." Maggot said "any."

2 **filmy:** eingetrübt. **grime:** Schmutz; Ruß. 10 **to brace oneself:** sich abstützen. 18 **bloodstain:** Blutfleck. 22 **bruise:** blauer Fleck.

Tears looked at me with big round brown eyes almost hidden by the straight black bangs that hung down her forehead. "Ever seen a dead person before?"

I didn't know. Sometimes it was hard to remember. "Yeah," I said, even though I wasn't sure.

"Ever *touch* a dead person before?" Maggot asked. I knew a dare when I heard one.

"Have you?" I asked back.

Maggot stepped closer to the body. Squatted down and placed his hand on Country Club's dirty forehead. Kept it there for a moment, then stood up and came back to us.

"What was it like?" Tears practically gasped. When you first saw her, she looked like she was around my age. She had a shape. But she acted young, and if you looked close it seemed like she was still growing. Like her eyes were too big for her round face. It gave her this always startled look. Like everything was a surprise.

"It was weird," Maggot answered. "I mean, his skin's cold to the touch. But that's not the only thing. You have to see for yourself."

Tears looked at me with those big dark little kid eyes. Like she wanted to know if she should do it. Or if I would.

I went over and squatted next to the body. By now I was

2 **bangs:** Ponyfrisur; Ponyfransen. 7 **dare:** Herausforderung. 9 **to squat down:** sich hinhocken. 12 **to gasp:** keuchen; hervorstoßen. 14 **shape:** Form; Figur. 18 **weird:** seltsam, merkwürdig.

pretty sure I never seen a dead person before. Never even been to a funeral. People said when you died you either went to Heaven or Hell. Maybe there really was a Hell because there was a show on TV about volcanoes, and it said that deep down inside the earth there was red-hot melted rock. But where was Heaven? People said it was up in the clouds. But what about the days when there were no clouds? Where was Heaven then?

Squatting close to Country Club's body in Piss Alley I looked up at the sky. All you could see were gray clouds above the tops of the buildings. Then I looked down at Country Club. Those blank, glassy eyes were staring straight up. "You lookin' for it, Country Club?" I whispered. "Let me know if you find it, okay?"

I reached down and put two fingers on his forehead. Maggot was right. It felt weird. The skin was cold and almost rubbery. I moved it a little with my finger. It didn't go back when I let go. On TV once I seen a man put his hand over the eyes of a dead person and close them. I put a finger on one of Country Club's eyelids and moved it down.

"Hey! What are you doing?" OG's shout caught me by surprise. OG didn't yell much, but when he did you saw the gaps where he was missing teeth and it made him look scary,

2 **funeral:** Begräbnis. 5 **red-hot:** glühend heiß. **melted rock:** geschmolzenes Gestein. 17 **rubbery:** gummiartig. 22 **to yell:** (an)schreien. 23 **scary:** Furcht einflößend.

like a witch or something. He picked up a beer can and threw it at me. It glanced off my forehead, but didn't hurt much because it was empty.

"Leave him alone, bitch!" OG screamed. I jumped back to where Maggot and Tears were.

"Gee, Maybe, don't you have any respect for the dead?" Maggot laughed.

OG picked up another beer can and threw it over our heads, yelling, "Get out of here! Leave us alone!"

Tears, Maggot, and me backed down the alley toward the street. We passed the shopping cart Country Club used to push around. It was full of rags and empty bottles. On top was a small black TV set with a dark green screen. It was broken, but in the reflection I could see back down the alley where OG was sitting next to Country Club. It was the last episode of the *OG and Country Club Show*. But maybe there would be a spin-off. *The Return of OG and Country Club*. Or maybe *Country Club in Heaven*.

"What'd it feel like?" Tears asked.

"What?" I was still watching the end of the *OG and Country Club Show.*

"Touching him."

"I don't know. Like a dead person."

1 **witch:** Hexe. 2 **to glance off:** abprallen. 10 **to back down:** zurückweichen. 11 **shopping cart:** Einkaufswagen. 12 **rags** (pl.)**:** Lumpen. 17 **spin-off:** Nachfolgesendung.

"Was he OG's best friend?" Tears asked.

"Yeah, they were close friends," Maggot said. "I think they'd been together for a long time."

Anyone else would have said, "they been together," but Maggot said, "they'd."

We stepped out of the alley and onto the sidewalk. People walked past wearing coats and hats, carrying briefcases and talking on cell phones, like it was any old day and there wasn't a dead guy a dozen yards away. Tears shoved her hands into the pockets of her gray sweatshirt. Except for the bangs that fell almost into her eyes, her black hair was short.

"Does it happen a lot?" she asked.

"OG throwing beer cans?" Maggot said.

"No, someone dying like that."

"All the time," Maggot said even though it was the first time I could remember. And I been around there since the summer. Longer than Maggot, who only showed up when the leaves on the trees were already starting to change colors.

"Don't it scare you?" Tears asked.

"Naw, Country Club was old," said Maggot.

"How old?"

"I don't know. Just old. Like in his twenties," Maggot said.

8 **cell phone:** Handy. **any old day:** ein Tag wie jeder andere. 18 **to show up:** auftauchen.

"You know he was lucky? A thousand years ago, like in the Dark Ages, you were lucky if you lived to be eighteen. Now everybody thinks they're supposed to live forever."

A woman in blue tights and a red down vest jogged toward us. Maggot held out a dirty hand. His fingernails were painted black. "Spare a little change, ma'am?"

"Sorry, don't have my wallet," the jogger answered.

"It's hard to think about living past eighteen," I said.

"Who'd want to?" added Maggot.

A police car came around the corner. Tears took off down the sidewalk and disappeared. The car stopped at the curb, and the cop in the passenger seat rolled down her window. She had streaked blond hair pulled back into a ponytail. I never seen her before, but I seen her partner, the one who was driving. His name was Officer Johnson and he was mean. He leaned toward the passenger-side window. "Hey, Maggot, what you dealin' today, oregano or baby powder?"

"Neither, Officer Johnson. I'm just out here spanging," Maggot answered. Spanging was street talk for spare-changing. "Hardly worth arresting me for. With the way our legal system works, I'll be back on the street before you can say misdemeanor."

"You got it all figured out, don't you, Maggot?" Officer

2 **Dark Ages:** finsteres Mittelalter. 4 **down vest:** Daunenjacke. 11 **curb:** Bordsteinkante 13 **streaked:** gestreift; meliert; mit Strähnchen. **ponytail:** Pferdeschwanz. 16 **mean:** fies. 22 **misdemeanor:** Vergehen, Übertretung. 23 **to figure s.th. out:** etwas begreifen, herausbekommen.

Johnson said with a smirk. The policewoman with the streaked hair just looked at us. The black nametag over her badge said Ryan.

"We got report of a dead body around here," Johnson said. "You kids know anything about that?"

Maggot gave me a look, then glanced at the entrance to Piss Alley. That was all it took. Officer Ryan got out of the patrol car and put on her dark blue police hat so the ponytail stuck out of the back. The hat looked too big for her head. She was about my height and not fat, but the thick black gun belt with the radio and gun and nightstick made her hips look wider than they really were. She looked down Piss Alley, then pulled the black radio off her belt and spoke into it. She hurried back to the patrol car and said something to Johnson, who was still inside. Then she rushed around to the trunk and got out an orange first aid kit and dashed back to the alley. You could kind of tell she was new. Maybe Country Club was the first dead person she ever seen, too. Or maybe she wasn't sure he was really dead. Meanwhile, Officer Johnson turned on the flashing lights and backed the car up so that it blocked the alley.

Just as they finished putting up the yellow crime scene tape, the orange-and-white EMS truck arrived, its siren blurping

1 **smirk:** (fieses) Grinsen. 2 **nametag:** Namensschild. 11 **nightstick:** Schlagstock. 15 **to rush:** hasten, rasen. 16 **trunk:** Kofferraum. 17 **to dash:** sausen, stürmen. 22 **crime scene tape:** Plastikband, mit dem der Ort eines Verbrechens abgesperrt wird. 23 **EMS truck:** Krankenwagen. (EMS: Abk. f. Emergency Medical Service).

and lights flashing. From down in Piss Alley came OG's raspy, liquid cough. Two EMS people with white shirts and dark pants got out of the truck and ducked under the crime scene tape and walked up to Officer Ryan. No one touched Country Club.

A crowd gathered on the sidewalk behind the crime scene tape. A green sedan pulled up. It had a flashing red light on the dashboard. Two men in dark suits got out and ducked under the tape.

"Detectives," Maggot said.

One of the detectives talked to Officer Ryan. The other told OG to get out of the alley. OG got up slowly and trudged away, the frayed bottoms of his jeans dragging along the ground. He was so skinny, his pants were always sliding off his hips. Went past us and down the street. The detective who had talked to Officer Ryan pulled on white latex gloves and began to feel around Country Club's body. The other one walked around the alley, looking at the ground and moving pieces of garbage with the tip of his shoe.

The two EMS people and Officer Ryan came back under the crime tape. The EMS people went to the ambulance and got a stretcher with wheels and a long black plasticbag with a zipper.

2 **raspy:** kratzig, krächzend. 3 **to duck under s.th.:** mit eingezogenem Kopf unter etwas hindurchgehen. 7 **sedan:** Limousine. 8 **dashboard:** Armaturenbrett. 12 **to trudge:** trotten. 13 **frayed bottom:** ausgefranstes unteres Ende. 22 **stretcher:** Tragbahre. 23 **zipper:** Reißverschluss.

"Think I could talk to you for a second?" Officer Ryan asked Maggot and me, flipping open a notepad.
"It's a free country for those who can afford it," Maggot replied. "First week on the job?"
Officer Ryan looked up and blinked. "How'd you know?"
"Lucky guess," Maggot said.
"Either of you know his real name?" Officer Ryan pointed her pen at Country Club.
We shook our heads.
"Where he came from?" she asked.
We shrugged.
Officer Johnson came over. He was a tall cop with a long face and a black moustache. "What are you doing?" he asked Officer Ryan.
"Trying to get some information," she answered.
"From them?" Johnson shook his head. "Don't waste your time."
Officer Ryan flipped her notepad closed and followed Johnson back to the patrol car.
"Hey," Maggot called behind them. "What'd he die of?"
"Exposure," Officer Johnson said over his shoulder without stopping.
"To what?" I asked.
"To the cold," Officer Johnson said as he pulled open the

2 **to flip open:** aufschlagen. **notepad:** Notizbuch. 5 **to blink:** blinzeln. 6 **guess:** Vermutung. 21 **exposure:** Aussetzung, etwas ausgesetzt sein.

car door. “To drugs, drink, disease, and hunger. Basically to life on the street. If you kids had any sense, you’d go home.”

“What if you don’t have a home to go to?” Maggot yelled back.

“You’ve got no parents, brothers, sisters, aunts, uncles, relatives?” asked Officer Ryan.

“You think I’d be living like this if I did?” Maggot said.

“You could go into a shelter.”

“No, thanks,” said Maggot. “Last time I spent a night in a shelter they robbed me of everything I had. I’d rather take my chances out here.”

“As long as you’re out here,” Officer Johnson said, “you don’t have a chance.”

5 **relatives:** Verwandte. 10 **to rob:** berauben, ausrauben.

THREE

It was the middle of the night and Rainbow, Tears, 2Moro, and me were out in front of the *Good Life Deli*. It was the only place still open. Not that we could go in since we didn't have no money. My stomach hurt and some food would have helped, but it was the deli's light we really needed. In the light we weren't gonna get rolled or cut or killed. The really bad ones, the junkies and weirdos who'd slit your throat as soon as look at you, they didn't like the light.

2Moro leaned against the wall, wearing black fishnet stockings and a short red dress and her orange and red patchwork jacket. She was smoking a cigarette. When she first showed up, her skin was this delicate olive tone, but it was more yellow now. Sometimes she forgot to go to the clinic to refill her HIV medications. Most days she spent more money on cigarettes than on food.

Rainbow sat against the wall with her eyes closed, wearing

13 **to get rolled:** ausgenommen, ausgeplündert werden. 14 **weirdo:** Verrückter. **to slit s.o.'s throat:** jdm. die Kehle aufschlitzen. 19 **delicate:** fein; zart. 21 **HIV medications:** Medikamente für HIV-Infizierte.

her black leather jacket with the collar turned up. She was nodding over, bending at the waist, her tangled blond hair falling into her lap.

"Why don't she just go to sleep?" Tears asked. Her breath was cloudy. We were wearing coats we found on the fence outside St. Marks Church, but we surely had no hats or gloves.

"She ain't sleepy," I answered.

"She can hardly keep her eyes open."

It was hard to believe Tears was so innocent.

"How old are you, really?" 2Moro asked.

"Sixteen."

"How come you run away every time the cops come around?"

"I don't know." Tears lifted her shoulders and let them drop. Under the dirt her pale skin looked smooth and soft.

"Listen, girl," 2Moro said, "I'm fifteen and you sure ain't no older than me. Tell the truth. What you afraid of?"

"Okay, I'm fourteen," Tears said.

"What year were you born?"

"Uh ..."

"If you're gonna lie, babe, you gotta be faster than that," Rainbow said without lifting her head. She did that all the

2 **to nod over:** einnicken. **to bend at the waist:** in der Taille einknicken.
10 **innocent:** unschuldig, naiv. 16 **smooth:** glatt.

time. Acted like she was totally out of it, but she was really right there, listening. "You're twelve, right?"

"I'll be thirteen in March."

"Where you from?" 2Moro asked.

Tears stared at her with those big round eyes.

"I thought you ain't supposed to tell," she replied.

"Who said?" Rainbow asked.

"Ain't it a rule?"

"We don't have rules," Rainbow said. "I come from North Miami Beach, Florida. Maybe, tell her where you come from."

"Uh, I don't know," I said.

"How can you not know where you're from?" Tears asked.

"It wasn't one place. It was all over."

"Maybe's mom was a carnie," Rainbow explained. "Traveled with a circus. What exactly your mom do, Maybe?"

"Lot of things," I said. "Sometimes she took care of the animals. Sometimes she was a clown. Put up and tore down the tents. Took the tickets for the freak show."

"This whole city's a freak show," 2Moro said.

Rainbow turned to Tears. "So where're you from?"

"Hundred, West Virginia."

"Hundred like hundred?" 2Moro teased.

6 **to be supposed to do s.th.:** etw. tun sollen. 15 **carnie:** Mitglied einer Zirkustruppe. 18 **to tear down:** abreißen. 19 **freak:** Missgeburt.

"Yes, it's called Hundred," Tears explained. "That's the name of the town, and it's in West Virginia."

"Why's it called that?" I asked.

"Everybody has a different answer," Tears said. "Some people say it's the speed limit or how long you have to count with your eyes closed to miss the whole town. Others say it's the average IQ."

"So what happened?" Rainbow asked. "What are you doing here?"

"Brent moved in."

"Let me guess," Rainbow said. "Your mom's new boyfriend? Or your new stepfather?"

Tears' eyes went wide. "Stepfather. How'd you know?"

"Happens all the time. So what'd he do? Start beating you?"

Tears shook her head. "He touched me. Mom would go to work and he put his hands inside my clothes. Said if I told her he'd say I asked him to do it."

"So you left?"

Tears' eyes got watery. "One day when Brent wasn't around I told her what he was doing. She didn't believe me. Said if it was true then I musta wanted him to do it. Then she called me a lot of names."

"So you ran away?"

5 **speed limit:** Geschwindigkeitsbegrenzung. 6 **to miss:** vermissen; verpassen. 19 **to get watery:** nass werden. 21 **musta:** *must have*. **to call s.o. names:** jnd. beschimpfen.

Tears shook her head again. The tears left streaks on her face. "I was scared. Didn't know where to go so I stayed. Only then it got worse. I guess Brent found out I told my mom and that she didn't believe me. So then he figured he could do anything he wanted. That's when I left."

"No aunts or uncles?" Rainbow asked.

"I got grandparents."

"Where are they?"

"In Hundred. But my grandpa got this disease. I think it's called Harkinson's or something. Makes him shake all over. So he can't feed himself or get dressed. My grandma has to take care of him. I asked my mom if I could go live with them, but she said no, they already got enough problems without me around."

A boxy white truck pulled up. It had a picture of a fish on the side. The driver got out. He was thin and wore a red baseball cap, a blue plaid shirt, jeans, and scuffed brown cowboy boots.

"Spare some change?" I asked as he crossed the sidewalk toward the *Good Life*.

He stopped and stared at me. People always stared the first time they saw me. "Why? So you can buy dope?"

I shook my head. "No, sir. Coffee and donuts."

15 **boxy:** kastenförmig. 17 **plaid:** kariert. **scuffed:** abgenutzt, abgewetzt. 22 **dope:** Stoff, Rauschgift.

He raised an eyebrow and went into the deli.

"My ears hurt it's so cold. Can't we go somewhere?" Tears put her hands over her ears to warm them.

"Where?" I asked.

"I don't know. Maybe we could find an unlocked car."

"No way," I warned her. "They find you in their car, they beat the crap out of you."

"Then what about –"

"Hush," I said, sensing something.

"What?"

"Someone's coming."

Tears looked down the sidewalk. Except for the streetlights it was dark and empty. "Where?"

If you lived on the street long enough you could sense things in the night before you saw them. A moment later a man appeared down the sidewalk. The leather soles of his shoes scraped lightly against the ground. He was wearing a long dark coat. His slacks were pressed to a sharp crease and his black hair was combed neatly back. Could have been just another person out late at night, but he wasn't. That's what you sensed. When they were looking for something.

He stopped in front of us and his eyes fixed on 2Moro. She slowly pushed herself away from the wall, and crushed her

1 **deli** (delicatessen): Feinkostgeschäft. 7 **to beat the crap out of s.o.:** jdn. zusammenschlagen. 9 **to sense s.th.:** etw. spüren. 18 **slacks:** Hose. **crease:** (Bügel-) Falte.

cigarette with the toe of her shoe. The man started to walk back the way he came, and she followed him into the dark not saying good-bye to us.

"I'm never gonna do that," Tears said. "Don't care how cold or hungry I am."

A siren wailed somewhere in the dark. In a building across the street, a light went on. Through the window I watched a bald man in a blue bathrobe pull open a refrigerator door and look inside.

"So what about you?" Tears asked me. "What are you doing here?"

"My mom told me to go."

"Why?"

"She drank up all the food money. I was the oldest and she said she couldn't afford to keep me around no more. Said I was the biggest so I had to go." It was worse than that, really. Way worse. But I didn't like to talk about it because then I had to remember.

"How come your skin's like that?" Tears asked.

My skin was a blotchy patchwork of dark and light color, like a dog with brown and white patches. A doctor told my mom it wasn't a disease; it was a "condition." The color in your skin is called pigment, and the pigment in my skin is

6 **to wail:** schluchzen, heulen. 8 **bald:** kahlköpfig. **refrigerator:** Kühlschrank. 17 **Way worse:** viel schlimmer. 20 **blotchy patchwork:** Fleckenteppich. 21 **patch:** Fleck. 22 **condition:** Zustand.

light brown. But I also have big patches where there's no pigment and the skin is whitish pink.

"It's just the way I was born," I said.

"Did you get into trouble a lot?" Tears asked next.

"Where?"

"With your mom."

"I tried to be good, but she was always mad at me anyway. Said I forgot to do this or I shouldn'ta done that. She wanted me to take care of the little ones. Feed 'em and clean 'em and stuff."

"Didn't you go to school?"

"I was supposed to, but most of the time we were too busy moving from one place to the next and she needed me to stay home to look after the kids. You ever take care of little kids?"

Tears shook her head.

"It's a pain. They don't stay still or do what they're told. My Mom said if I didn't do a good job she was gonna have to find someone else to take care of them. Said she couldn't afford to take care of me if I couldn't pull my own weight. Said it would be best if I just went away."

"How many were there?" Tears asked.

"She got four besides me. All littler."

8 **shouldn'ta:** *should not have.* 9 **and stuff:** und so. 20 **to pull one's weight:** seinen Anteil dazutun.

"Do you miss them?"

"One or two. I'm the only one who's all mixed up colors." And the only one with a scar on her back from being burned with a hot iron.

The door to the *Good Life* swung open and the guy with the red baseball cap came out. He was carrying a gray cardboard tray with four white paper cups filled with coffee and a white paper bag of donuts neatly folded over at the top.

"Where's your friend?" he asked, counting only Rainbow, Tears, and me.

"She had to go somewhere," I answered.

"Well, here you go." He handed me the tray and bag and turned toward the truck.

"That's it?" I asked. "You don't want nothing in return?"

He stopped. "You gonna listen if I tell you to stop taking drugs or go home to your parents?"

Tears and me didn't answer. The truck driver touched the brim of his cap. "I'll look for you the next time I come through. That is, if any of you are still here."

3 **scar:** Narbe. 4 **iron:** Bügeleisen 5 **to swing open:** aufschwingen. 7 **tray:** Tablett. 8 **neatly:** sorgfältig. 18 **brim:** Rand.

FOUR

The building had dull sheets of metal where the windows once were and a black metal door locked with a chain across it. Scaffolding rose up the front and a big blue Dumpster sat at the curb. During the day workmen were fixing it up. At night the building was empty. We stood in the rain while OG pulled a metal sheet off a window. It was dark inside. We lit candles in a big room on the second floor. The air inside was damp and chilled, but at least we were dry. From other rooms we dragged in an old mattress, some broken chairs, and an upside-down pail to sit on. Here and there patches of yellow wallpaper clung to the walls, and Maggot covered them with black spray-painted signs of anarchy, a circle with a capital A inside, and his tag, CLASS WAR, in big black letters.

Rainbow lay on the mattress, wrapped in a tattered pink baby quilt she'd found in the garbage. The quilt had bunny

8 **sheet:** Platte. 10 **scaffolding:** Gerüst. **Dumpster:** Müllcontainer. 15 **chilled:** gekühlt. 17 **pail:** Eimer. 20 **tag:** Signatur eines Sprayers. 23 **quilt:** Steppdecke, Bettdecke.

rabbits on it, and white stuffing leaked out of rips. Rainbow's eyes were closed. I sat on the corner of the mattress and watched a candle's flickering light dance on her soft, pale skin. A strand of blond hair fell across her eyes. Rainbow was the only kid I knew whose blond hair was real. I thought she was the most beautiful person I ever seen.

In another corner, 2Moro and Jewel were on their knees in front of a big shard of broken mirror propped against the wall. Small bunches of candles on the floor provided light. It looked kind of religious. Like in a church. All together, the candles made enough light to cast huge, hulking shadows of 2Moro and Jewel against the far wall.

Under her patchwork jacket 2Moro was wearing a tight purple tank top, a short black leather skirt, fishnet stockings, and leather boots. Her bright red hair stood up straight.

Next to her Jewel patted rouge onto his dark cheeks. He'd dyed his hair Manic Panic Purple and the highlights shined in the candlelight. He wore a long black leather coat and under it black pants and a white shirt.

"You finished with the eyeliner?" he asked 2Moro.

"Almost," she answered.

"Don't be a hog," he said.

1 **stuffing:** Füllmaterial **rip:** Riss. 8 **shard:** Scherbe. **propped against:** angelehnt an. 14 **tank top:** ärmelloses Top. 18 **dyed:** gefärbt. **highlights:** Strähnen. 23 **hog:** Schwein; Egoist.

2Moro sighed. "Go put on lipstick.".

"First I want to wait to see how the eyeliner looks," Jewel said.

"Then you gonna have to wait."

"Did you take your pills today?" Jewel asked. Every day 2Moro was supposed to take eight pills for her HIV.

"Get lost."

"The doctor at the clinic said if you don't take those pills, it's going to turn into AIDS."

2Moro rolled her eyes and ignored him.

Jewel's cell phone rang. He reached into his small black leather handbag and took it out. "Hello?" he answered in a singsong voice. "Oh, hi, Suzy. I'm home getting ready for tonight. What? She's on TV right now? Oh, God, I'd love to see her, but my little brother's watching and he's such a monster. Another TV? Oh, sure, we've got lots of them, but you know, that means going to a whole other floor and this house is just too big. So you'll tell me all about it when I see you at the club, okay? Great. Sure I have your number in my cell phone. Has its own melody. *Crazy in Love*. See you later. Ciao!"

Jewel snapped the cell phone shut. He had no TV. Or little brother. Or house. No one knew where he got the cell phone.

7 **Get lost:** leck mich am Arsch. 22 **to snap shut:** zuklappen.

Maybe from some rich club kid who couldn't be bothered to report it missing.

On the mattress Rainbow had opened her eyes and propped her head on her hand. The tattered sleeve of her leather jacket slid down to her elbow. Her forearm was covered with long thin scars and scabs where she cut herself. "Who was that you were lying to?" she asked with a yawn.

"Oh, look who came out of her trance," Jewel said. "That was Suzy Herman, my new love."

"How many TVs does *she* have?" Rainbow asked.

"Not just TVs, my dear. Houses. Real estate. What you will. Her parents have an estate in Greenwich, a beach house in East Hampton, and a ski condo in Sun Bird."

"It's Snowbird, you dimwit," Maggot muttered.

"Whatever," Jewel replied with a huff. "I'm not supposed to tell anyone this, but her father *owns* Vaseline."

Everyone got quiet. Finally Rainbow said, "In a tube or a jar?"

"The company, you ninny," Jewel said. "I mean, think about all the Vaseline in the world, and he owns it."

"I guess that makes him a pretty slick businessman," Maggot said, and laughed all by himself.

"You are such a bore, Maggot," Jewel said.

1 **to bother:** sich die Mühe machen. 4 **tattered:** zerlumpt, zerfetzt. 12 **estate:** Anwesen. 13 **ski condo:** luxuriöse Skihütte. 14 **dimwit:** Schwachkopf. 15 **with a huff:** eingeschnappt. 19 **ninny:** Dussel. 21 **slick:** glitschig; gewieft, clever. 23 **bore:** Langweiler.

"I'd rather be a bore than a tramp," Maggot shot back.

"And so crude," said Jewel. "Anyway, Suzy's father gave her an apartment and a Mercedes. And, for your information, we are going to get married, and then I'm going to be rich, too."

"Yeah, right, White wedding. With a carriage drawn by four horses. All the rich and famous invited," OG grumbled from the corner where he was sitting in a broken chair, rolling a cigarette. I was surprised to hear his voice. It was the first time he spoke since Country Club died.

"What do *you* know?" Jewel stuck his nose in the air.

OG coughed and wheezed. "Look around the room, man. Look at who you're with. You can't get there from here."

"*You* can't because you're a smelly, scuzzy crusty," Jewel said. "I can get anywhere I want and be anyone I want." He picked up a short blue skirt and held it against his hips, then wiggled suggestively. "I have class. We may not have beds but we wear fashionable threads. Maybe I'll be a Revlon cover girl."

"Would Suzy want to marry a girl?" Tears asked.

"No," answered Jewel. "I'll be a boy for her."

"And a cover girl for Revlon," Maggot snickered.

Suddenly we heard voices. Grown up voices. We went quiet

2 **crude:** ordinär. 12 **to wheeze:** einen pfeifenden Atem haben. 14 **scuzzy crusty:** dreckiger Punk. 16 **hips:** Hüften. 17 **to wiggle suggestively:** aufreizend wackeln. 19 **cover girl:** Mädchen auf dem Titelblatt einer Zeitschrift.

and alert like rabbits prick up their ears and birds lift their heads.

"Blow out the candles," OG whispered.

Jewel and 2Moro put out the candles. The room went dark. Now that the rain had slowed, we could hear the city sounds of car horns and the wheezing of air brakes on buses. We listened. There were bad people in the night. Creeps who liked to hurt kids. Psychos who set drunks on fire and watched them burn. Weirdoes who knew that if they killed a homeless kid there was a good chance no one would ever know, and an even better chance that no one would care.

The voices we heard that night sounded official, like teachers or police. Through the doorway we saw the round spot of a flashlight beam strike the wall at the top of the stairs. The voices were clearer now. One was male, the other was female.

"Smell the candles?"

"And spray paint. It's fresh. Someone's up here."

"I think there's a group of them."

A second flashlight beam joined the first. They reached the second floor landing and the beams swept into the room where we crouched in the dark. I counted two dark silhouettes in the doorway. Couldn't see their faces, only that they were both about the same height.

1 **alert:** hellwach. 6 **car horn:** Hupe. 7 **creep:** Widerling. 8 **psycho:** Psychopath. 14 **flashlight beam:** Lichtstrahl einer Taschenlampe.

The beams swept over Maggot and Rainbow and Jewel and 2Moro. Tears was hiding somewhere in the shadows or in another room. OG must have worked hard not to cough, because now that they had found us, he went into a spasm of hacking. When the flashlight beam found me, it stayed longer than on the others, as if the person holding the light couldn't quite tell what he was seeing. I shielded my eyes.

"What do you want?" Maggot asked.

"We want to give you a warm meal and a safe place to spend the night," the female flashlight figure answered.

"What do you want in return?" Maggot asked.

"In return for what?" asked the male flashlight.

"Giving us food and a place to sleep."

"Nothing," answered the male flashlight figure.

"We're from the Youth Housing Project," added the female flashlight.

"That mean I can't come?" asked OG.

"How old are you?" asked the male flashlight.

"Twenty-two," OG answered.

"It's only for kids eighteen and under," said the female flashlight. "But we can take you to a shelter where you can get medical attention."

A match burst into light, and 2Moro's face brightened as

4 **to go into a spasm of hacking:** einen Hustenanfall bekommen. 7 **to shield:** (mit der Hand oder dem Arm) schützen. 11 **in return:** als Gegenleistung. 22 **to get medical attention:** medizinisch versorgt werden.

she leaned toward the flame with a cigarette between her lips. The tip glowed red as she inhaled and blew the match out with a stream of smoke. "Can I smoke there?"

"You can smoke outside the facility if you have to," the female flashlight answered.

"Maybe I *want* to," 2Moro said.

"Even though it'll kill you?" the female flashlight asked.

"I'm HIV positive, lady," 2Moro shot back. "Plenty else gonna kill me before cigarettes."

"How do you handle the issue of alcohol?" Maggot asked.

"No drugs or alcohol allowed," said the male flashlight. His voice was harsher now that he saw that Maggot was putting him on.

"So there is something you want," Maggot concluded. "You'll give us food and a bed, but only if we live by your rules."

"It's only fair," said the female flashlight.

"What's fair about it?" 2Moro asked. "Who are you to tell us how to live?"

"Cigarettes and alcohol are bad for you," the female flashlight continued.

"Look, I don't really care if you want to smoke and drink," the male flashlight added. "But if we allow that at the project, the state will take away our funding."

2 **tip:** Spitze. 4 **facility:** Einrichtung. 12 **harsh:** rau; schroff. **to put s.o. on:** jdn. aufziehen. 24 **funding:** Mittel, Gelder.

"Now, I understand. So we have to live by the state's rules?" Maggot smirked. "Javohl! Heil Hitler! We love you, Saddam. Raise your red flags, comrades! The state rules!"

"We're only looking out for your safety and welfare," the female flashlight said ignoring Maggot's outburst. "The longer you stay on the street, the better the chance you'll die before the age of thirty."

"Thirty?" Maggot laughed. "Forget it. I won't live past eighteen."

"Do you know that every day fourteen children are buried in unmarked graves because no one knows who they are?" the woman asked. "Do you want to be one of them? You could die and no one would ever know. Your parents would never know. Do you really want that?"

"Sounds okay to me," said 2Moro.

"Couldn't agree more," agreed Maggot. "By the way, what makes you think our parents even care?"

"Of course they do," the female flashlight insisted.

"Then why did my parents tell me to get out and never come back?" Jewel asked.

"My mom don't want me back," added Rainbow. "Not unless I can get her drugs or money."

"Blaming your parents for your crappy lives isn't going to

4 **welfare:** Wohlergehen. 5 **outburst:** Ausbruch. 11 **unmarked grave:** anonymes Grab. 23 **to blame s.o.:** jdn. verantwortlich machen. **crappy:** beschissen.

help," the male flashlight said. "You have to help yourselves. We're offering the first step. We'll get you off the street and cleaned up."

"And then what?" OG asked.

"Then it's nine to five," Maggot said. "The status quo. God, Mom, apple pie, and the good old American capitalist patriarchic society."

"You'd rather stay here?" the female flashlight asked, sounding disappointed.

"Why not," answered Rainbow. "If this is what it takes to be free and do what we want and come and go as we please without a bunch of goody-two-shoe grown-ups telling us what we can and can't do."

It got quiet. The sounds of the city crept back into the room. The man and woman lowered their flashlights so that the beams lit the floor. A crushed beer can here. An empty noodle packet there. 2Moro puffed on her cigarette and the ember glowed red in the dim light.

"Thanks for stopping by." OG waved like he expected the flashlight people would finally give up and go away.

"The temperature's supposed to drop below freezing tonight and then down into the teens by the end of the week," the male flashlight said. "It's going to get awful cold in here."

5 **status quo:** Status Quo, gegenwärtiger Zustand. 12 **bunch:** Haufen **goody-two-shoe grown-ups:** tugendhafte (spießige) Erwachsene. 18 **ember:** Glut. 21 **to drop below freezing:** unter den Gefrierpunkt fallen. 22 **into the teens:** zwischen 10 und 20 Grad Fahrenheit (ca. -12 bis -7 Grad Celsius).

"Thanks for the weather forecast," Maggot smirked.

"You'd really rather live like this?" the woman flashlight asked again.

"Hey, remember that old song by Janis Joplin about freedom being just another word for nothing left to lose?" OG asked, then went into another spasm of coughing.

The male flashlight ignored him. "You realize some of you may not be alive by this time next year?"

"Is that a promise?" Maggot asked.

With a loud sigh, the male flashlight turned to the female. "Let's go."

The female flashlight had one last thing to say. "I know it's hard for you to talk to us with your friends around, but you can always come by yourself and they won't know. Remember, it's the Youth Housing Project on St. Marks Place."

The flashlights turned away and went back down the stairs. The room went dark. Then small flames burst on as 2Moro began to relight the candles.

"Someday I'm going to live in a penthouse," Jewel said. "And I'll go find those two and invite them up for a drink."

18 **to relight:** wieder anzünden. 19 **penthouse:** Penthouse, Dachterassenwohnung.

FIVE

It got colder. I saw a lady fall on the icy sidewalk. Coffee froze solid if you left it overnight in a cup. My stomach hurt. There was stuff at the drug store to make it feel better, but it cost money. I found a piece of cardboard in the garbage and a pen lying in the street. I made a sign:

MONY 4 EGS AN CRAONS

I stood on the sidewalk outside the food store and showed the sign to the people who came out carrying big bags of groceries, but they all stared at my face, then the sign, then frowned and kept walking. After a while, Jewel came by wearing a short black jacket and a tight black skirt and boots.

"What's that supposed to say, Maybe?" he asked.

"Money for eggs and crayons."

10 **stuff:** Zeug. 18 **groceries:** Lebensmittel. 22 **what's that supposed to say?:** was soll das heißen? 23 **crayon:** Buntstift.

Jewel laughed. "Oh, my dear, you are priceless! Do you have anything to write with?"

I still had the pen I found. Jewel took it and changed my sign. "There. That's better. Didn't they teach you to spell in school?"

"What school?" I asked.

"You never went to school?"

"Here and there, but never for long."

A man came out of the store carrying a white plastic shopping bag in each hand. He looked at me and my sign. "Eggs, huh?" He put down the bags and took out four eggs. Then a lady came out and gave me some, too.

Now I needed crayons. I crossed out the eggs part of my sign and stood outside a store that sold newspapers and candy and postcards. A woman came out with two little kids. She had smooth blond hair and wore a long blue coat with brown fur at the collar and the ends of the sleeves. The kids were blond with matching pink barrettes in their hair. They wore matching denim jackets over matching white sweaters. One of the kids pointed at me. "Mommy, look."

The woman put her hands on their shoulders and tried to steer them away. "Come on, let's go this way."

But the kids didn't want to go.

1 **priceless:** unbezahlbar. 17 **fur:** Pelz. 18 **matching:** zusammenpassend. **barrette:** Haarspange. 19 **sweater:** Pullover, Sweatshirt. 21 **to steer away:** weglotsen.

"What's wrong with her face?" one asked.

"What does she want?" asked the other.

"Nothing," the woman said. "I want you to come."

But the kids kept staring. "What does that say?"

"I need crayons," I said.

The kids were so cute. Their mouths became circles. "We have crayons, Mommy!"

"I want you to come right now," the woman said sharply. "Do not talk to that person."

"Why?" asked one of the kids.

"Just don't!" The woman took each kid by the hand and yanked them away.

I stayed outside the store until a man came out. He was wearing a white shirt and a brown tie, but no jacket. "Go away," he said.

"You don't own the sidewalk," I said. That was what Maggot always said when they told him to move.

"You're hurting my business," he said. "Customers won't come in with you standing here."

I shrugged like I didn't care.

The man went back into the store and came out with a small box of crayons. "Now go away."

That's what I did.

6 **cute:** niedlich. 12 **to yank away:** wegreißen. 20 **to shrug:** mit den Schultern zucken. **like I didn't care:** als ob es mir egal wäre.

You have to color the eggs carefully. Crayons get hard when it's cold, and if you press too much on the shells they break. It was getting dark when I finished coloring them. I went to a movie theater near Central Park. At night in New York, people stand on lines waiting to get in. They wait in the rain and snow and cold. They talk to their friends and drink coffee. I stood on the sidewalk near the line of people and started to juggle the eggs.

When I was little, a man who liked my mom taught me to juggle. I don't remember his name. He said I was a good juggler for my age because I could keep four balls going at once. The people who ran the circus found out and sometimes they dressed me up like a clown and let me juggle in the circus. People would clap and laugh. They liked to see a little kid juggle. My mom liked it because she got extra money when I juggled. She liked me then.

But I got older and they stopped letting me juggle. Mom said people who came to the circus expected a kid who was twelve to do better tricks than I could do. But it was different outside the movie theater. I didn't have to be so good. I just had to get people to watch me.

"I bet you're wondering which egg will fall and break first," I said when they were watching. "The red one? The blue? Maybe the yellow or the orange."

2 **shell:** Schale, Hülle. 8 **to juggle:** jonglieren. 14 **to clap:** klatschen.

"Or maybe none of them," someone in the line called back.

"What if I start to do tricks?" I asked, tossing one of the eggs up and catching it behind my back while I juggled the other three in front of me.

"One of them will surely break," someone said.

"Want to bet which one?" I asked.

"Whichever one we bet on will be the one you let drop," someone said.

"Not if you don't bet me," I told them. "You bet each other. I just get one of the bets. The winner gets the other two."

"So you need four people to bet," one of them realized. "One for each color."

"I'll bet a dollar on yellow," said a man smoking a cigar.

"I'll bet on red," said a woman wearing a bright red ski jacket.

"A dollar ain't much," I said. "How about making it two?"

"How do we know it's not rigged?" asked the man with the cigar. "How do we know you're not in cahoots with one of the bettors and you'll split the winnings, too?"

"Oh, sure, you all hang out with street urchins like me," I said. Maggot told me to use the word *urchin*. I wasn't sure what it meant, but it made people laugh.

"I know how we can tell if it's not rigged," said the man

2 **to toss:** werfen. 6 **to bet:** wetten. 17 **rigged:** getürkt, manipuliert. 18 **to be in cahoots with s.o.:** mit jdm. unter einer Decke stecken. 19 **bettor:** Wettender. **to split the winnings:** den Gewinn aufteilen. 20 **street urchin:** Gassenkind.

with the cigar. "Only people who bought a movie ticket can bet. No one's gonna spend ten bucks on a ticket so they can make four bucks on a bet, right?"

"Good point," said the woman in the red ski jacket. She and the man with the cigar held up their tickets. Two more people quickly joined the betting. I started doing harder tricks behind my back and under my leg. Finally, the red one broke. The woman in the ski jacket won. Two of the bettors paid her. The man with the cigar paid me.

"Let's do it again," he said. "This time for five bucks."

Except for him, the other bettors were new. I started juggling again with another red egg. I always brought two of each color.

This time the yellow one broke. The man with the cigar won. Two of the bettors gave him five dollars, but the man who was supposed to give five to me refused.

"I think this is a scam," he said to the man with the cigar. "It's no coincidence that you suggested we up the bet to five bucks and that's when you won."

"You really think I'm in cahoots with that kid?" The man with the cigar pointed at me.

"I don't know, but I'm definitely not paying," the other man said. The line began to move. People started going into the

4 **good point:** das stimmt allerdings. 6 **harder tricks:** schwierigere Kunststücke. 16 **to refuse:** sich weigern. 17 **scam:** Betrug. 18 **coincidence:** Zufall. **to up the bet:** die Wette erhöhen.

theater. The man who was supposed to pay me followed the line.

"Would you give me one of the bets you won?" I asked the man with the cigar.

"Sorry, kid," he answered. "You said I'd get two of the bets. That's what I got. What's fair is fair." He went into the theater.

I still had enough eggs for one more bet so I waited for another line to form. And once again people took the bets. I dropped the last red one and made $4 for the night.

I took the subway back to St. Marks Place wondering if I had enough money for the stomach medicine. People passed in heavy coats and hats. Some even wore scarves. Up ahead a bunch of kids sat on a stoop under a light, smoking and talking. They were mostly wearing black clothes and had tattoos and piercings. I seen some of them around before and knew they were mean.

I decided to cross the street, but then someone called out, "Hey, Maybe." It was Rainbow. She was one of the kids sitting on the steps. "Come over here, okay?"

The other kids gave me mean smiles but I went over. A boy with a pointy orange Mohawk muttered something under his breath that I couldn't hear. The other kids laughed.

13 **up ahead:** weiter die Straße runter. 14 **stoop:** Treppe. 22 **pointy:** spitz zulaufend. **Mohawk:** Irokesenschnitt. **to mutter something under one's breath:** etwas murmeln.

"Where you coming from?" Rainbow asked when I got close. She was chewing gum.

"The movies."

"Oh, yeah, what'd you see?" asked the boy with the orange Mohawk.

"Nothing. I was juggling."

"Maybe does this thing with colored eggs." Rainbow told the group how I got people to bet and shared in some of the winnings. "So how much did you make?"

"Only four dollars."

"Whatcha gonna do with it?" Rainbow asked me.

"Buy some medicine for my stomach," I said.

"Know what my mom used to do when I had a stomachache?" Rainbow said. "Gave me ginger ale. It always made me feel better. Your mom ever give you ginger ale for your stomach?"

I shook my head. I didn't remember having stomachaches when I was with my mom. Maybe I did. But I didn't remember.

"You ought to try it," Rainbow said. "Maybe you could keep two bucks for the ginger ale and give the rest to me, huh?"

"You need money?" I asked.

8 **to share in the winnings:** einen Anteil vom Gewinn bekommen. 13 **stomachache:** Magenschmerzen. 21 **buck:** Dollar.

"Oh, yeah," Rainbow said. "You know me. I *always* need money."

I knew a bottle of ginger ale would not cost more than two dollars. If Rainbow needed money I was glad to give the rest to her.

4 **to be glad:** sich freuen.

SIX

The ginger ale worked for a little while, but then my stomach started to hurt again. I spent the night with Tears, Maggot, and OG in the empty building. Jewel and 2Moro were clubbing and Rainbow stayed out all night. Maggot had a furry white toy dog he stole from a store. It yipped and did back flips. He named it Killer and pretended he was teaching it tricks.

"Okay, Killer, this time I want you to bark and do a back flip." He flicked the switch on Killer's tummy and the toy dog did exactly what it was told.

"Good dog!" Maggot cheered. "Now let's see if you can do it again."

The toy did it again. Maggot scooped it up into his arms. "What a good little dog. Let daddy give you a hug."

Tears and I laughed and laughed, and I forgot about my stomachache. OG sat in a corner drinking from a bottle, but

11 (to go) **clubbing:** durch Nachtclubs ziehen. 12 **to yip:** kläffen. 13 **back flip:** Überschlag rückwärts. 16 **tummy:** Bauch. 21 **hug:** Umarmung.

even he showed his gap-toothed grin a few times. The funny thing about Maggot was that he was the reason we were all together, and he didn't even know it. It happened back in the fall, on a windy night when the dead leaves made scratching sounds as they skidded and bounced down the street. OG and Country Club were sitting against the wall outside the *Good Life* sharing a bottle in a brown paper bag. A dozen feet away Rainbow was nodding against the same wall. I spanged enough change to buy coffee and was sitting with her. Back then Rainbow and I hardly knew each other. We met the day before when a man from a restaurant gave me a bag of day-old bread and Rainbow asked if she could have some.

We had seen OG and Country Club around but never talked to them. They were older and crusty and stuck to themselves. Anyway, I was next to Rainbow, sipping my coffee, when out of the dark came Maggot carrying a green Army-surplus backpack. He stopped on the sidewalk, sort of half way between OG and Country Club and Rainbow and me. "You guys have a place to stay tonight?" He swiveled his head from Rainbow and me to OG and Country Club. I guess he thought we were all together.

"You're lookin' at it," OG said.

1 **gap:** Lücke. 2 **reason:** Grund. 4 **fall:** Herbst. 5 **to skid:** schliddern, rutschen. **to bounce:** hüpfen. 17 **Army-surplus backpack:** Rucksack aus Armeebeständen. 20 **to swivel:** drehen.

"Mind if I hang with you?" Maggot asked.

"Be our guest," said Country Club.

So Maggot sat down between Rainbow and me and OG and Country Club. He started asking us questions, like where we were from and how long we been living on the streets. From then on we started hanging together. A few weeks later Rainbow ran into 2Moro and Jewel at the clinic, and they started hanging with us, too.

And now it was winter, and we were sort of like a family, or maybe a tribe. An asphalt tribe that roamed the streets searching for food and shelter. We watched out for each other, cared about each other. Country Club was gone, but the rest of us stuck together.

The next day the sun came out. People were wearing sweaters or open jackets.

"Today is a perfect day to sell some Ecstasy," Maggot announced. "Anyone want to come?"

"Can we buy some medicine for my stomach?" I asked. It was hurting again.

"Sure, Maybe, we'll get you anything you want."

Maggot and Tears and me walked over to Tomkins Square Park. The sun was slanting toward the west giving the dark leafless trees long shadows, so it was probably late after-

6 **to hang together:** zusammen rumhängen. 10 **tribe:** Stamm. 13 **to stick together:** zusammenhalten. 16 **to announce:** verkünden. 22 **to slant:** schief stehen, sich neigen.

noon. The park was surrounded by a black metal fence that came up to my chin. The police locked it at midnight but people could still climb over. The metal gates were open now. Since it was a warm, sunny day for winter, a lot of people came outside to sit and feel the sun. Old ladies in shawls sat next to Goths wearing black lipstick and eye shadow. An old man wearing a gray hat threw bread crumbs to a flock of clucking pigeons that scrambled around at his feet. Other men sat at small square concrete tables and played chess. Young couples pushed babies in strollers and walked dogs. An artist with big pieces of chalk sketched a trampoline-size painting on the asphalt playground. A policeman on a bicycle rode by.

Tears and I sat down on a bench while Maggot went off to sell.

"What's Ecstasy?" Tears asked.

I tried not to stare at her. Sometimes it was hard to believe how innocent she was. Who didn't know about Ecstasy?

"What was the name of that place you come from?" I asked.

"Hundred," she answered.

"You sure it's not a Million?" I teased. "Like a million miles from anywhere?"

Tears pursed her lips like I'd hurt her feelings.

6 **Goths:** Grufties. 7 **flock:** Schar. 8 **clucking pigeons:** gurrende Tauben. 10 **stroller:** Kinderwagen. **to walk the dog:** mit dem Hund Gassi gehen. 23 **to purse one's lips:** schmollen.

I rubbed my shoulder against hers. "Hey, I'm just kidding. Ecstasy is a club drug. It makes people happy."

"Is it against the law?"

"Yeah."

"Can't Maggot get into trouble if the police catch him?"

"He ain't selling real Ecstasy," I said.

Tears scowled but didn't ask nothing more.

We heard a scratching sound. "Up there." Tears pointed at a tree overhead. A small gray squirrel was scrambling up the trunk. When it got to the top branches it let out a long, mournful cry and then started back down.

"I think it's looking for its mommy," Tears said.

The little squirrel reached the ground, then started up the next tree. Tears and I watched as it got to the top and let out another mournful cry. Animals may all sound different, but you always know when they're crying.

"That's sad," Tears said.

The sun dipped lower. The shadows of buildings spread over us like a cold gray blanket. I started to shiver. Tears pulled her bulky brown coat tight around her neck. "What's taking Maggot so long?" she asked.

I shrugged. Across the walk the little squirrel started up another tree.

3 **against the law:** gegen das Gesetz. 5 **to get into trouble:** Ärger bekommen. 7 **to scowl:** ein finsteres Gesicht machen. 9 **squirrel:** Eichhörnchen. **to scramble up:** hochklettern. 11 **mournful:** traurig. 20 **bulky:** unförmig.

"It already went up that tree," Tears said.

"Maybe it don't know what else to do," I said.

Maggot trotted down the path laughing. "Come on, we better get out of here."

We got up and followed him out of the park. On the way Maggot told us he sold aspirin to some tourists for $60.

"They think they bought Ecstasy," he chuckled. "They'll go clubbing tonight. At least they won't have to worry about getting a headache."

He stopped talking and slowed down. We were on the sidewalk now. Up ahead a bunch of kids with tattoos and piercings were hanging out on the corner. Some of them were the kids I'd seen with Rainbow the previous night. I hoped she was there.

"Hey, look, it's Lost," Maggot said. "He's always got roofies."

Maggot went to talk to the one named Lost, the one with the orange-tipped Mohawk who made fun of me the night before. I looked for Rainbow.

"Lookin' for your girlfriend?" one of the other boys asked me.

"Maybe," I said.

"You maybe got some more money for her?" He held out

3 **path:** Weg. 8 **to worry:** sich Sorgen machen. 13 **previous:** vorangegangen. 15 **roofies:** starkes Schlafmittel (KO-Droge).

his hand. The fingernails were long and had black crescents of dirt under them. "You can give it to me. I'll see her later and give it to her."

I backed away. Maggot and Lost had their hands in their pockets. Maggot pulled out a bunch of bills and gave them to Lost, who handed him a plastic baggie filled with white pills.

"Oh-oh," said the boy with the dirty fingernails. "Now that Maggot's got them roofies, your girlfriend's gonna like him more than you."

I didn't like what he was saying, but I didn't dare to speak up. Maggot put the baggie in his pocket and came back to Tears and me. "Come on, let's go." He was so excited.

"I gotta say this for capitalism," Maggot said. "It's a great system if you know how to manipulate it. You start with about twenty-five cents' worth of aspirins and convert that into sixty bucks worth of roofies which I'll sell at *The Cradle* tonight for a hundred and eighty."

"You can't get into *The Cradle*," Tears said. "It's the hottest club in the world."

Maggot patted his pocket. "I can with these."

"What about my stomach medicine?" I asked.

"Aw, crap." Maggot's shoulders slumped. "I forgot. I'm sorry, Maybe. All I have now are these roofies. But I'll sell

1 **crescent:** Halbmond. 6 **baggie:** Tütchen. 13 **excited:** aufgeregt. 16 **to convert:** umwandeln. 23 **Aw, crap:** ach, Scheiße.

them tonight and tomorrow I'll have plenty of money, okay? We'll get you that medicine then."

My stomach hurt bad. I thought about that little squirrel climbing tree after tree and crying. Bet his stomach hurt, too.

1 **plenty of money:** reichlich Geld.

SEVEN

"I'm so gross! I'm disgusting! I can't stand it!" Rainbow laughed crazily as she pulled me down the block.

"You look beautiful to me," I said.

"Oh, Maybe, what would you know? You're even smellier and dirtier than me."

"I am?" Even though I knew that all of us street kids were dirty and smelly, it still made me feel somewhat bad to hear Rainbow say it. That wasn't the way I wanted her to think of me.

"Aw, look, I hurt your feelings." Rainbow stuck out her lower lip and pouted. "I'm sorry, Maybe. But I'm dirty and smelly, too. We're the dirty and smelly twins!" She hooked her arm through mine and started to skip. I tried to keep up with her. It made me happy when she wanted to be with me. Then she let go and did a cartwheel right in the middle of the sidewalk. The regular people looked at her like she was psycho.

8 **gross:** fett; widerlich. **disgusting:** ekelhaft. **I can't stand it:** ich halt's nicht aus. 18 **to pout:** schmollen. 22 **to do a cartwheel:** Rad schlagen.

"What?" she dusted off her hands and yelled at them. "You never seen someone do a cartwheel before?"

The regular people cut a wide circle around her and didn't answer.

"Jerks," Rainbow muttered.

"Where did you go this morning?" I asked. She usually didn't get up until the afternoon, but that day she was gone early.

"2Moro and I went to the clinic for our meds," she said in a singsong voice. "I got Ritalin and Prozac. I'm ADD and bipolar and OCD and XYZ. And you know what happens if I take it all at once? I'm off my tree!" She ran toward a light pole, grabbed it, and swung around. Then she came back, panting for breath. "Come on, Maybe, let's get ourselves cleaned up."

"Where?"

"There." Rainbow pointed at a low building. The reddish-brown bricks were covered with a layer of gray grime, but the big windows in front were clear and clean. Inside, people sat at rows of computers. Beyond them were lots of shelves filled with books.

"It's a library," I realized.

1 **to yell at s.o.:** jdn. anschreien. 5 **jerk:** Idiot. 9 **meds:** (medications) Medikamente. 10 **Ritalin:** Medikament gegen Hyperaktivität. **Prozac:** Medikament gegen Depressionen. **ADD:** hyperaktiv. 11 **bipolar:** manisch-depressiv. **OCD:** zwangsneurotisch. **XYZ:** XYZ (*ironisch gemeint*). 12 **I'm off my tree:** ich heb total ab. 13 **light pole:** Laternenpfahl.

"There's no getting anything past you, Maybe." Rainbow started up the steps toward the doors.

"You sure we're allowed?" I asked.

"It's open to the public. Just like the bus station."

"Don't you need a card?"

"Only if you want to take books out," she said and pushed on the door. We went in and through a kind of metal detector. Some grown men and women stood behind a wooden counter with computers and stacks of books on it. They wore plastic photo IDs and gave us unfriendly looks. A woman in a blue dress wrinkled her nose and fanned her face with her hand.

We passed the tables with the computers on them. All kinds of people were sitting there. Old men, mothers with babies on their laps, kids. A tall thin man with a photo ID and short, curly reddish hair walked around behind the computers and talked to anyone who needed help. I stopped and stared. He had a broad, flat nose and patchy skin like mine. Only the patches with pigment were lighter and spotted with reddish freckles. Like me, the patches without pigment were plain milky white. He was wearing neatly pressed khaki slacks and a blue shirt. "Come on, it's probably over this way." Rainbow tugged at my sleeve and led me past the

9 **stack of books:** Bücherstapel. 10 **ID:** Ausweis. 11 **to fan:** (be-)fächeln. 18 **patchy:** fleckig. 19 **spotted with:** getüpfelt, gefleckt. 20 **freckles:** Sommersprossen. 22 **khaki slacks:** Khakihose. 23 **to tug:** ziehen, zerren. **sleeve:** Ärmel.

shelves of books toward the back where there was a men's room and a women's room. We went into the women's room.

"Down here." Rainbow held open the door to the big handicapped stall at the end of the bathroom. I went in and Rainbow slid the latch closed. She took off her leather jacket and hung it on the hook inside the door. Then she started to take off her clothes and put them on the toilet seat. Her arms and legs were covered with those long thin scars and scabs. I knew she cut herself, but I never seen her do it. She saw me looking.

"Sorry," I said and looked away.

She looked down at herself and shrugged, then back at me. "What are you waiting for?"

I slowly stripped off my clothes and put them on the toilet seat with Rainbow's. It was chilly in the bathroom, and I felt goose bumps rise on my skin. It felt strange and frightening to be naked in a public place. But together with Rainbow also a little daring and exciting.

Now it was Rainbow's turn to stare at me. "Wow, I never seen nothing like you."

I looked down at myself. My whole body was covered with light and dark patches. "I'm ugly."

4 **handicapped stall:** Kabine für Behinderte. 6 **to slide the latch closed:** den Riegel vorschieben. 16 **chilly:** kalt, frostig. 17 **goose bumps:** Gänsehaut. 19 **daring:** gewagt.

Rainbow pursed her lips and frowned. “No. Just different.” She went to the stall door and undid the latch. “Ready?”

“Uh huh.”

We scampered over to the row of sinks and mirrors, took brown paper towels from the dispenser and wet them with hot water from the faucet. Then we squeezed the pink liquid soap onto them and ran back to the stall. Rainbow closed the latch and we soaped ourselves down. The warm sudsy paper towels felt good on my skin except for the places where I had sores that stung from the soap. I rubbed the towels down my arms and was shocked to see how much lighter the skin became.

“Surprised?” Rainbow asked.

“I didn’t know how dirty I was,” I answered.

She laughed. The mud-colored water dripped from our elbows and ran down our legs. Soon the tile floor in the stall was covered with soggy, filthy paper towels. We left the stall again. Back at the sinks I held down the hot-and cold-water knobs while Rainbow washed her hair under the faucet, using the liquid soap. Brown water disappeared down the drain. Then it was my turn. The counter and floor around the sinks grew slippery, and our wet, soapy feet slid on the smooth tile floor.

4 **to scamper:** flitzen. 5 **dispenser:** Papierspender. **to wet:** befeuchten. 6 **faucet:** Hahn. 8 **sudsy:** schaumig. 10 **sore:** wunde Stelle. 16 **tile floor:** Kachelfußboden. **soggy:** durchnässt. 18 **sink:** Waschbecken. 19 **knob:** Knopf. 21 **drain:** Abfluss. 22 **slippery:** rutschig.

"Shouldn't we go back to the stall?" I asked when I finished washing my hair. The hot water felt good as it dripped down onto my shoulders and arms.

"It's too slippery," Rainbow said. "Let's stay here. Do my back?"

She turned around and I started to scrub her back with a soapy paper towel. I didn't ask about the green, brown, and yellow bruises on her arms and legs and sides.

"Now mine?" I asked when I finished her back. I leaned over a sink and put my elbows on the counter and waited to feel the hot towels. Nothing happened. I looked over my shoulder. Rainbow was staring at my back.

"An iron?" Her voice was soft.

I nodded.

"Shit," she muttered. A moment later I felt hot water run down my sides. The water tickled when it ran down the insides of my naked legs. It felt good to have someone wash me. The bathroom door squeaked. Rainbow and me looked up. A woman came in with a little girl, maybe four or five years old. The little girl's hair was braided into pigtails and she was wearing a pink sweatshirt that said Princess in glittering silver letters. She was wearing jeans and white tennis shoes with pink laces. She was so perfect. So clean and her

13 **iron:** Bügeleisen. 16 **to tickle:** kitzeln. 18 **to squeak:** quietschen. 20 **braided into pigtails:** in Zöpfe geflochten.

clothes so neat and new. Even when I lived with my mom I never was that neat and clean.

The woman gasped and the little girl stared with bulging eyes. Without a word the woman pulled her out of the bathroom.

"We better go." Rainbow's voice turned serious. Leaning over the sinks we began to rinse the soap off our bodies. Water splashed all over the counter. We started to dry ourselves. The coarse towels were rough against our skin. A few of the scabs on Rainbow's arms and legs got rubbed away and started to bleed a little, but somehow she didn't seem to care.

I looked at myself in the water-splattered mirror. I was someone with curly brown matted-down wet hair. Someone whose skin was pale pink in some places and splotchy brown in others. So thin her ribs and collarbone stuck out. Shoulders and arms angular and bony.

"I hate putting those dirty clothes back on," Rainbow muttered, rubbing paper towels down her bruised legs.

"Maybe we should leave them," I said, "and go through the library naked."

"Or like this." Rainbow pressed brown paper towels against her breasts so that they stuck. I giggled at the thought of us

3 **bulging eyes:** Glotzaugen. 15 **splotchy:** fleckig. 16 **collarbone:** Schlüsselbein. 17 **angular:** knochig, hager. 23 **to giggle:** kichern.

covered like that and walking past the people with the ID tags.

Then the bathroom door opened again.

And two men came in.

EIGHT

The short chubby one had wavy black hair and was wearing a blue security guard's uniform. The other one was tall and broad-shouldered with short brown hair and a cigarette stuck behind one ear. He was wearing jeans and a gray shirt with "Bobby" stitched in red letters over the pocket.

"What the hell?" the one named Bobby growled. "Who's gonna clean up this mess?"

Rainbow and I retreated toward the back wall, covering our naked bodies with our hands.

"Lock the door," Bobby told the chubby security guard.

"You sure?" the guard asked nervously.

"Yeah, I'm sure," Bobby snapped. "*You* want to clean up this mess? 'Cause I don't. And no one can use this place the way it is now."

I heard a click as the guard locked the door. Bobby pulled a ring of keys from his belt and opened another door, this one

1 **chubby:** pummelig, rundlich. 2 **security guard:** Wachmann. 13 **to growl:** knurren. 14 **mess:** Schweinerei. 19 **to snap:** anschnauzen.

to a supply closet. He wheeled out a pail with a long wooden mop handle sticking up from it, then put his foot on the edge of the pail and kicked it across the floor toward Rainbow and me. We jumped out of the way and it banged against the wall.

"Get to work," he snarled, then reached into the closet again and tossed a roll of black plastic garbage bags at us. Rainbow and I were trapped. Still covering our naked bodies with our hands, we started to inch toward the handicapped stall.

"Where do you think you're going?" Bobby demanded.

"To get our clothes," Rainbow answered.

A nasty leer crept through Bobby's lips. "Naw, that ain't no fun. You get to work the way you are."

Rainbow and I kept inching toward the stall.

"Hey!" Bobby shouted and started toward us. His work boots skidded on the slimy paper towels, and he lost his balance and started to flail around, swinging his arms wildly to keep from falling. Rainbow and I grinned.

Bang! Bobby got his balance back and slammed the stall door with his fist. The sound made Rainbow and me jump. "Think that was funny?" He yelled, coming closer. "Come

1 **supply closet:** Vorratsschrank. 2 **mop handle:** Griffstange eines (Nass-)Mops. 6 **to snarl:** knurren. 9 **to inch towards s.th.:** sich langsam (zollweise) auf etw. zubewegen. 13 **nasty leer:** bösartiges, anzügliches Grinsen. 16 **to start towards s.o.:** auf jdn. zukommen. 17 **to lose one's balance:** das Gleichgewicht verlieren. 18 **to flail around:** rudernde Armbewegungen machen.

here, you freak." He grabbed me by the hair and yanked down, pulling me off my feet. I hit the hard, wet tile floor with my knees and elbows. It hurt bad.

"Now get to work!" he said, then pointed at Rainbow. "You, too!"

"Hey, Bobby, come on," said the security guard.

"Naw, you come on," Bobby yelled back. "Unless *you* wanna clean up this mess."

"They should do it," said the security guard. "I just don't see why you have to hurt 'em."

"You don't teach 'em a lesson, they'll come back and do it again," Bobby said.

"They're just a couple of street kids."

"You don't like it, why don't you get out?" Bobby snapped. "Put that sign on the door that says bathroom temporarily out of order."

Without another word, the security guard left. Bobby followed him to the door and locked it. He turned back to Rainbow and me. "What're you lookin' at? Get back to work."

Rainbow and me got on our hands and knees on the floor, scooped up the wet, dirty paper towels and dumped them into a big black plastic bag. We were still naked.

"Damn street punks always coming in here and messing the

15 **temporarily** (adv.): vorübergehend. 16 **out of order:** außer Betrieb.
22 **to scoop up:** aufschaufeln.

place up," Bobby grumbled. He stood over us. I was afraid to look up, lest he start yelling again. But as I picked up the paper towels, I watched his scuffed work boots, ready to back away if they turned in my direction.

"Sluts. Lousy pieces of crap," Bobby muttered. Rainbow and I worked silently, afraid to say or do anything that might make Bobby angrier. Before long we'd gotten all the wet paper towels off the wet floor.

"In there, too." Bobby ordered, and pointed into the handicapped stall. Me and Rainbow hesitated. It was one thing to be on our hands and knees out in the bathroom, but another to do that inside the stall.

"Go on!" Bobby yelled.

"Can't we use a broom or something?" I asked.

The answer was the grooved bottom of Bobby's work boot on my bare behind and then a hard shove sending me toward the stall. My hands slipped out from under me, and my chin and chest slid along wet floor.

"Teach you sluts to come in here and mess this place up," Bobby growled. He stepped into the stall and kicked our clothes off the toilet seat.

I pushed myself back up to my hands and knees in the dirty, soapy slop. Inside the disabled stall the floor smelled like

5 **slut:** Schlampe. 10 **to hesitate:** zögern. 15 **grooved bottom:** gerillte Sohle. 16 **bare behind:** nackter Hintern. 19 (that will) **teach you:** das wird euch eine Lehre sein. **to mess up:** verdrecken.

Piss Alley. My chin and elbows hurt and I felt the old trembling sensation of wanting to cry. When I was little it would blow through me like a gust of wet wind. I could never stop it. It would sweep in, and I would cry whether I wanted to or not. But as I got older I learned to fight it. When they – my mom, her boyfriends, and other kids – called me names and hurt me, I wasn't strong enough to hit back, but I would clench my teeth and blink hard to stop the tears. As long as I didn't cry, I won in a way. So I fought it and sooner or later it would pass like a dark cloud that don't rain. Then after a while I forgot the feeling altogether. Or maybe it just went away. It was a long time since I cried. So when the feeling came back after Bobby shoved me with his foot into the stall and I fell forward and banged my chin and elbows, it caught me by surprise. I felt it take hold and waited for the tears to come. But they didn't. The feeling came and went without touching the place that brought the tears. And I wondered if maybe that place had gone away forever and would never come back.

Dragging the plastic garbage bag, Rainbow crawled into the stall and started to pick up the paper towels.

"You don't have to do this," I whispered.

She didn't answer. Her eyes were empty, and she moved like

3 **gust of wind:** Windbö. 4 **to sweep in:** hereinfegen. 8 **to clench one's teeth:** die Zähne zusammenbeißen. **to blink hard:** immer wieder blinzeln. 13 **to shove:** schubsen. 20 **to drag:** ziehen. **garbage bag:** Müllbeutel.

a zombie. Like she wasn't there. We picked up the slimy, wet paper towels, but the floor was still covered with the dirty, soapy water. Our clothes lay in a pile in it.

"Okay, get up!" Bobby barked.

Rainbow and I stood up, again covering ourselves with our hands. Bobby pointed at me. "You mop." He pointed at Rainbow. "You do the counter and the mirror." He went back to the supply closet and got a big sponge, some paper towels and a bottle of Windex. These he put on the counter for Rainbow.

To do what he wanted, we had to stand up and use our hands. It wasn't like when we were down on the floor. Then Bobby couldn't see much. Now he could see everything. I felt his eyes – staring mostly at Rainbow's naked body, but every now and then at mine. I didn't care. Let him look all he wanted. It didn't matter. Nothing mattered except getting out of there.

I swept the stringy mop across the floor. Soon it was soaked and wouldn't pick up no more water. I gave Bobby a puzzled look.

"Wring it out, stupid," he snorted. "Don't you know how to use a mop?"

I held the mop over the bucket and twisted the long bunched

8 **sponge:** Schwamm. 9 **Windex:** Fensterputzmittel. 18 **soaked:** patschnass. 19 **puzzled look:** verwirrter Blick. 23 **to twist:** drehen. **bunched up strings:** Fadenbüschel.

up strings with my hands the way I once seen my mom do it. Cold, brown water dribbled into the bucket.

"Not like that, you ugly freak." Bobby ripped the mop out of my hands. He put it into a metal thing in the pail and pushed down on a short handle. Brown water gushed through holes in the metal thing and splashed into the pail. "Got it now?"

I took the mop. Nothing Bobby said could really hurt me. Nothing he did could hurt for long, neither. I heard it all before. Been hurt plenty all my life. Like when my mom used to say I was a mistake she wished never happened. She had all those kids and no money and she got fat and men came and left. The men would leave and she couldn't hurt them so she hurt me instead. It was something grown-ups thought they had a right to do. When they got angry they could find some kid, someone smaller, and hurt him or her. What could a kid do? Nothing, except run away.

Rainbow finished cleaning the counter and mirrors about the same time I finished mopping the floor. "Aw, hell, I can't stand watchin' you two anymore," Bobby grumbled. "What a crap job. Look at the streaks all over those mirrors. There's still dirt all over the floor. I'm gonna have to redo the whole thing myself. Get your clothes and get the hell out."

2 **to dribble:** tropfen. 5 **to gush:** schießen. 6 **to splash:** spritzen. 22 **to redo:** etwas nochmals machen.

Rainbow and me went back to the handicapped stall. Our dirty clothes were lying in a damp heap on the floor. Who wanted to put on wet filthy clothes that have been lying next to the toilet? But we had no choice, and slowly pulled them on. They smelled awful. The last thing Rainbow did was pull her leather jacket on over her wet, dirty sweatshirt.

"Get out." Bobby went to the bathroom door and unlocked it. The chubby security guard was outside. He stared at Rainbow and me in our soggy, stained clothes. We headed for the front.

"Not that way," Bobby hissed from behind and herded us to the right, past the guard and toward a door that said PERSONNEL ONLY. The door opened to a hall. It was some kind of storage area, lined with shelves filled with books and videotapes. At the end of the hall was another door with a big red exit sign over it. Rainbow and I pushed through the door. The chilly gray air outside was sudden and unexpected. I guess for a little while in there I forgot it was winter. Now the cold air cut through our wet clothes and stung our faces. We were in a small parking lot behind the library. I felt a hand in the middle of my back. Then I was sailing forward. I hit the asphalt and skidded on my face and hands

9 **stained:** befleckt. **to head for:** eine Richtung auf etw. einschlagen. 11 **to hiss:** zischen. **to herd:** treiben. 12 **personnel:** Personal. 13 **some kind of:** eine Art. 14 **storage area:** Lager. 22 **to hit the asphalt:** auf den Asphalt knallen.

and knees. Next to me Rainbow let out a cry, then lay still on the cold, rough parking lot.

"You think this was bad?" Bobby growled. "I see you two here again, you'll *really* be sorry."

We slowly got to our feet. A long scrape ran from Rainbow's cheekbone to her jaw. The tiny beads of blood were spreading and running together. My face burned like fire. I could see the scratches on my palms and feel the ones where the knees of my jeans had torn. The cold air crept in through every buttonhole and sleeve and tear, coiling inside my wet clothes like a snake. One more thing that wanted to hurt us.

6 **cheekbone:** Wangenknochen. 8 **palm:** Handfläche. 10 **buttonhole:** Knopfloch.

NINE

Now that Country Club was dead, OG got a little brown puppy with long floppy ears, white paws, and a white streak like a bolt of lightning on its chest. OG called him Pest. Pest only wanted to play tug of war. He bit the legs of our pants, or the sleeves of our sweatshirts and pulled and growled playfully.

OG and me sat on the sidewalk in front of the bakery with Maggot who was spanging with a cardboard sign that read:

MONEY FOR MARYJUANA.

Grrrrrrrrr! Pest's little teeth were clamped on the rope OG used as a leash. The little dog growled and shook his head, pulling as hard as he could. It was funny to see a puppy act so ferociously.

"What happened to your face?" OG asked me.

9 **puppy:** junger Hund. **paws:** Pfoten. 10 **bolt of lightning:** Blitz. 11 **tug of war:** Tauziehen. 19 **rope:** Seil, Strick. 20 **leash:** Leine. 22 **ferociously** (adv.): wild.

A long brown scab went from my left eye to my jaw.

"Someone pushed me," I said.

"You push back?" Maggot asked.

I didn't answer.

Grrrrrrrrr! Pest kept yanking at the leash. Each time he did, he yanked OG's arm, too. OG went into a coughing fit, one hand covering his mouth and the other holding the leash. He coughed so hard his whole body shook.

"Okay, Pest, that's enough," he croaked as he tried to catch his breath.

Grrrrrrrrr! Pest kept pulling. He didn't understand what OG was saying. He probably thought coughing was a human bark.

"I said that's enough." OG wheezed. He coughed something red into his hand and wiped it on the ground.

Grrrrrrrrr!

OG jerked the leash hard, pulling Pest off his feet. The puppy hit the sidewalk with a yelp, then cowered with his tail between his legs. "Aw, puppy." OG instantly felt bad for losing his temper. He gathered the frightened little dog into his arms and hugged him. Pest started to lick OG's face. No matter how bad you hurt a puppy, it still loved you. Not like human beings.

6 **coughing fit:** Hustenanfall. 9 **to croak:** krächzen. 20 **to lose one's temper:** die Beherrschung verlieren. 21 **to hug:** umarmen.

A couple stopped on the sidewalk. With their long coats they appeared very tall to me. They were both carrying briefcases – bet they were doing big business.

"Are you serious?" the man asked, nodding at Maggot's "Money For Maryjuana" sign.

"Why not?" Maggot answered. "If the sign said, 'Money For food', would you believe it? Least I'm honest."

"At least you ought to spell it right," said the woman.

Maggot turned the sign around and looked at it. "I spelled 'money' wrong?"

The man smiled. "He's got a sense of humor."

"Not for long if I don't score some pot," Maggot warned them.

The woman put on a teacher's expression. "You're smart. Why do you live like this? Why don't you clean yourself up and get off the street?"

"Maybe I don't want to," Maggot answered. "Maybe I'd rather live on the street than have to get some stupid nine-to-five job."

"But at least you'd have a warm place to live and clean clothes," said the woman.

"Where does it say that everyone has to wear clean clothes?" Maggot asked. "Where does it say everyone has to have a

2 **briefcase:** Aktentasche. 7 **least:** *at least.* 12 **to score:** bekommen. **pot:** Marihuana.

warm place to live? Maybe I don't want any of that crap. Maybe I'm happy being dirty and homeless and free of possessions and responsibilities. Who the hell are you to tell me how to live?"

The man reached for the woman's elbow. "I think we should go, Rachel."

But Rachel didn't budge. "You remind me of my brother."

"Oh, yeah? He a street punk too?" Maggot asked.

"No, he's in college."

OG laughed, then started to cough. Rachel and her male friend glared at him, then Rachel looked back at Maggot. "What I meant was, he's rebellious like you. He questions everything."

"He raises his hand in class," joked OG.

Rachel ignored that and said to Maggot, "I am quite sure, you'd like him."

Maggot smiled up at her, but I knew he thought she was crazy. Like we street kids had anything in common with someone in college.

"Does he know about the revolution?" Maggot asked.

The man knit his brows. "What revolution?"

"The revolution that's gonna start when people wake up and realize that the government floods ghettos and slums

2 **possession:** Besitz. 3 **responsibility:** Verantwortung. 7 **to budge:** sich rühren. 11 **to glare at:** zornig anstarren. 21 **to knit one's brows:** die Stirn runzeln.

with drugs to keep all the poor and oppressed people stoned and complacent so they don't rebel."

"If you believe that, why are you begging for drug money?" asked Rachel.

"Might as well enjoy it while I can." Maggot grinned.

"We really better get going, Rachel," said the man.

"Wait." Rachel opened her bag and started to hunt around in it.

"You're not serious," her friend sputtered. "You know he's going to use it for drugs."

"That's his choice," Rachel answered defiantly and pulled out a black wallet. The man looked around nervously, like expecting a gang of homeless kids to jump them.

Rachel took a $5 bill and held it just out of Maggot's reach. "I want you to promise me that you'll think about what I said. You don't have to live like this."

Maggot looked up at her like a puppy. It must have been hard for him not to snatch the bill out of her fingers.

"Promise?" Rachel asked.

"I promise." Maggot took the bill from her. Rachel turned to her friend, who shook his head like he couldn't believe what she done. Together they went off down the sidewalk. Maggot held the $5 bill flat and tight between his fingers.

1 **to flood ... with drugs:** mit Drogen überfluten. **oppressed:** unterdrückt. **stoned:** unter Drogen stehend. 2 **complacent:** selbstzufrieden, apathisch. 5 **to enjoy:** genießen, 7 **to hunt around:** herumsuchen. 11 **defiantly** (adv.): trotzig; herausfordernd.

"Worked like a charm. The sign pulls them in, but you know what really ices the deal? Spelling marijuana wrong. It brings out all their middle-class guilt about the poor getting a crap education."

"You gonna keep your promise?" OG teased.

"I promise ..." Maggot heaved himself up to his feet, "to go find Lost right now. Later, compadres."

"Hey, bring something back for us," OG called after him, then started to cough again.

"Sure," Maggot called back over his shoulder with a laugh. "I promise."

1 **charm:** Zauber. 7 **compadres** (spanisch): Genossen.

TEN

Since the "Money For Maryjuana" sign worked for Maggot, I tried it next. Pest squirmed out of OG's arms and wanted to play again, so OG tied the rope to his backpack and Pest played tug of war with that instead. He growled and pulled but couldn't get the backpack to budge. Then Tears came along dragging a clear plastic garbage bag half-filled with yellow and red McDonald's cups and napkins and other garbage.

We tore open the bag and dug into the food, picking out mushy French fries, cheeseburgers with just two or three bites taken out of them, and tall waxy cups with a few ounces of soda left in the bottoms. The smell of food filled the air.

Tears alternated between the straw from the cup in her right hand and the straw from the cup in her left hand. "Iced tea. Lemonade. Iced tea. Lemonade. I can't decide which I like better."

17 **mushy:** matschig. **French fries:** Pommes Frites. 18 **waxy:** wächsern.
21 **to alternate:** abwechseln. **straw:** Strohhalm.

"Mix them," I said.

She pried off the plastic caps and poured them together, then took a big sip. "Perfect!"

"I told them to hold the pickles," OG joked, using his dirty fingers to pull a slice of green pickle out of a half-eaten bun. Pest barked and wagged his tail eagerly. OG tore off a piece of hamburger and fed it to him.

I found half a Big Mac and bit into it. White sauce dripped down my hands and onto my pants. From the first bite my stomach growled like it was angry that I forgot to feed it for the past few days.

"Whose dog is that?"

We looked up to find a woman with frizzy red hair standing over us. She was wearing a gray sweatshirt that said PETA.

"He's mine." OG put his hands around Pest and drew him close.

"You shouldn't be feeding him garbage," the woman said.

"It's good garbage," I said, holding up a partly eaten Big Mac. A clump of lettuce fell onto the sidewalk. Just to gross out the woman, I picked it up and put it in my mouth. "Good enough for humans."

Tears raised her hand like she was in school. "What's PETA?"

2 **to pry off:** abmachen. 4 **to hold the pickles:** nicht so viele Mixed Pickles (in Essig eingelegte Gemüsestücke) dazugeben. 5 **bun:** Brötchen. 13 **frizzy:** kraus. 19 **clump of lettuce:** Salatklumpen. **to gross out s.o.:** jdn. durch sein Verhalten anekeln.

"People for the Ethical Treatment of Animals," the woman answered and looked back at OG.

"Has he had his shots?" she demanded.

Whatever answer OG started to give was lost in a spasm of coughing.

"Have you?" Tears asked. I never seen her talk back to a grown-up before. She was learning to be a street kid.

"Of course he hasn't had his shots." The woman answered her own question. "You can't even take care of yourselves, much less a pet. Is he fixed?"

"Get lost," OG croaked between coughs.

"You shouldn't be allowed to have animals," the woman said. "You don't know how to take care of them."

"He'll do a better job than you," I said.

The woman glared furiously at me. "That's such nonsense. Look at what he's feeding him."

"He loves him," I said. "You don't love nothing."

"How would you know?" the PETA woman asked. She stared at me more closely.

"Don't worry," I said. "I'm fixed and I had my shots."

The woman frowned, then turned back to OG. "Someone should take that dog away and give it a good home. It's just going to die out here on the street."

"Officer Johnson says everything dies on the street," I said.

3 **shots:** Impfungen. 10 **fixed:** kastriert. 14 **to do a good job:** etw. gut machen, gute Arbeit leisten.

The woman ignored me. "If you really love that dog you should give it to me. I'll find a good home for it."
"Go away!" OG cuddled Pest more tightly.
The woman made a face. "You're all sick."
She stood there waiting for one of us to say something, but no one spoke. It was no use. People like her never listened. They made up their minds, told you what they thought, and that was the end of it. Finally she left. Pest yelped and struggled to get free, but OG held him close like he was afraid to let the little dog go until the woman was well out of sight.
"How comes she cares so much about a dog?" Tears asked. "What about us?"
"Nobody cares about us," I said.

3 **to cuddle:** in den Arm nehmen, schmusen. **tightly** (adv.): fest. 4 **to make a face:** das Gesicht verziehen. 6 **to be no use:** nichts nützen. 7 **to make up one's mind:** sich entscheiden, eine Meinung bilden.

ELEVEN

Rainbow was gone for days and I got worried. She didn't usually disappear for that long. I waited until night and then went to look for her. The air was cold and damp, and my breath came out in big clouds of white. I headed for the streets near Lincoln Tunnel where men in cars prowled for young girls and boys they drove home to their families in the suburbs. I was walking down a dark sidewalk when a sleek silver car pulled alongside of me.

The window on the passenger side went down. "Hey," a man's voice said. In the dark shadows of the car I could see that he was old. The lines around his mouth were deep and the hair on his head was so thin that unless you looked close you might think he was bald. He looked small for a grown-up. Not much bigger than me.

"You look hungry," he said. There was something mean about his smile. Like he knew he had what I needed and it

9 **to disappear:** verschwinden. 12 **to prowl:** auf Streifzug sein. 14 **suburb:** Vorort. 15 **to pull alongside:** seitlich heranfahren. 22 **mean:** gemein, fies.

was simply a matter of reeling me in. He was wearing a tan-colored jacket with a green corduroy collar. It looked warm. All I had on was a T-shirt and a thin sweatshirt. I left my jacket somewhere, but I couldn't remember where.

"Maybe." I shivered, and my empty stomach churned like a washing machine with no clothes in it.

"Looks like you could use a bath, too."

"Maybe." It had been a week since me and Rainbow washed in the library bathroom, but I was already filthy again. My hands were almost black with dirt. My arms and face were streaked with it. I could taste it when I licked my lips. My hair was caked. When I scratched my head my scalp felt like it was full of sand.

"Why don't you come with me?" the guy offered. "I'll give you something to eat. And a bath."

"What do you get in return?" I asked.

He grinned in the darkness. "I guess we'll have to see."

I heard a tap. Then another and another. A fat raindrop landed on my head. Another hit my ear. I felt a chill. The taps began to come faster as the big drops of rain pelted the sidewalk and me. I started to walk. The car moved along slowly.

1 **to reel in:** (Netz) einholen. **tan-coloured:** hellbraun. 2 **corduroy collar:** Kragen aus Cord. 5 **to churn:** wirbeln, sich wild drehen. 12 **caked:** verfilzt. **to scratch:** kratzen. **scalp:** Kopfhaut. 19 **to feel a chill:** frösteln.

"You really want to stay out here in the rain tonight?" the man in the car asked. "You'll probably catch pneumonia."

"Maybe." I was already cold. Shivers ran up my back and arms, and I clenched my teeth so that he wouldn't hear them chatter.

"So you coming or not?"

I didn't answer.

The guy looked angry. The rain was starting to go into his car through the open window. "What are you waiting for?" he asked. "Money? Forget it. I'm not giving you any money. I'll feed you and clean you up. But I know what you'll do if I give you money. You'll just spend it on drugs."

"Maybe."

He narrowed his eyes. "You'd rather stay out here and freeze and starve and be filthy? Fine. There are a dozen kids just like you on these streets. You don't want to come with me, I'll find another one. What's the difference? You're all the same, know that?"

"Maybe."

"Maybe ... Maybe ..." he repeated. "Maybe you'll starve or freeze to death out here tonight. Maybe in the morning they'll find your body. Who'll miss a homeless kid? You know what you are? You're a waste. Not even a memory. Just someone who never was."

2 **pneumonia:** Lungenentzündung. 5 **to chatter** (teeth): mit den Zähnen klappern. 14 **to freeze:** frieren. 15 **to starve:** hungern. 22 **body:** Leiche.

The car window went up. The windshield wipers began to swipe back and forth as the man drove away down the dark wet street. I stood in the rain, feeling the drops hit my head and shoulders. He could find some other hungry gutter punk who wanted to get out of the rain. But it wouldn't be me.

1 **windshield wipers:** Scheibenwischer. 2 **to swipe back and forth:** hin und her wischen. 4 **gutter punk:** Gossenkind.

TWELVE

I spent most of the night walking the streets around the tunnel looking for Rainbow, then slept for a while in a 24-hour banking room where people came in and got money from ATMs. Toward morning the rain turned to snow and a brown security truck stopped at the curb. A security guard came in and kicked me out of the ATM room. Outside, the dark, snow-covered streets were empty. Skinny white icicles hung from the streetlights.

I walked down town. The hood of my sweatshirt froze stiff and turned white with snow. I was cold, but I liked being outside. As morning came the darkness turned to a dull gray. For once the city was quiet and pretty. Hardly anyone was out. The streets were white, and all the storefronts were covered with metal gates and grates. The only footprints down the sidewalk were mine.

Soon the cold seeped deep into me. My teeth chattered. My

11 **ATM:** Geldautomat. 14 **icicle:** Eiszapfen. 16 **hood:** Kaputze. 19 **for once:** ausnahmsweise einmal. 20 **storefront:** Vorderseite eines Geschäfts. 21 **grate:** Gitter. 23 **to seep:** sickern.

feet were numb and each step I took hurt. My fingers grew stiff and throbbed with pain. Up ahead was that brick building with the big windows. The library – a warm, dry place that was open to the public. But all I could think about was that mean creep Bobby. As I passed the building I looked in through the windows. It was dark inside. I could see the tables with all those computers that anyone could use. The chairs were empty and the computer screens were blank. No sign of Bobby, but that didn't mean he wasn't in there somewhere.

"Hello." Coming toward me was someone wearing a long brown coat and a fuzzy cap of blue, red, and yellow wool. He was tall and carried two big shopping bags. It was the man who had blotchy skin like mine. We stared at each other.

"Vitiligo," he said.

"What?"

He pressed a finger against a pale patch on his chin. "That's what this is called. Have you always had it?"

I nodded.

"Me, too," he said. "Did you want to get into the library?"

I didn't answer. I was confused. I thought he'd say more about our skin. But he acted like it was no big deal. Like it

1 **numb:** taub. 2 **to throb with pain:** vor Schmerz pochen. 12 **fuzzy:** flaumig, wuschelig. 23 **he acted like it was no big deal:** er tat so, als sei das nichts Besonderes.

was the same as two people who were both left-handed or had green eyes. Then I looked in the shopping bags he was carrying. They were filled with paper plates and napkins and plastic cups. I could smell donuts.

"Well, I'm afraid it's too early. We won't be open for a few hours," he said. Then he cocked his head and looked more closely at me. "You're shivering."

"Maybe."

"What's your name?"

"Maybe."

He made a funny face. "I see, Maybe. Maybe. Well, Maybe, we're having a Martin Luther King celebration today. I came in early to set up. If you'd like to come in now you can get warm and I'll give you something to eat."

"What about Bobby?"

The man frowned. "How do you know Bobby?"

"The other day he hurt me and my friend."

"That was you? Tony told me what Bobby did."

"Who?"

"Tony's the security guard," he explained. "I want you to know that you're welcome to come in here any time you want and you will not be hurt. I'll make sure Bobby leaves you alone. Of course, you'd be better off washing some-

3 **napkin:** Serviette. 6 **to cock one's head:** den Kopf schief legen. 7 **to shiver:** zittern. 16 **to frown:** die Stirn runzeln. 23 **you'd be better off:** es wäre besser, wenn du … **someplace else:** woanders.

place else. If you need a place to do that, I can probably help you. Bobby won't be here until later. No need to worry. You can come in now and get warm and have something to eat."

He sounded sincere, like one of the nice ones. But you never knew. He might still want something. Everyone wanted something. He went past me and up the snow-covered steps, then took out some keys and opened the door. He looked back. "Still not coming?"

I wanted to so bad.

"You can eat and get warm and go. No one will hurt you."

I followed him through the front doors, but stopped inside where the air felt dry and warm. I stayed close to the doors. Just in case.

"You can wait here if you want," the man said, leaving the shopping bags by the computer tables and going toward the back. I waited, still shaking from the cold outside, my stomach churning hungrily at the thought of food so close.

It seemed like a long time before he came back, but it probably wasn't that long.

"That sweatshirt's all wet," he said. "Why don't you take it off, and I'll put it on the radiator to dry."

I pulled the sweatshirt over my head. The hood and shoulders were soaked dark. The man held it with the tips of his fingers.

4 **sincere:** aufrichtig. 9 **so bad:** so sehr. 13 **just in case:** nur um auf Nummer sicher zu gehen. 21 **radiator:** Heizkörper. 23 **soaked dark:** dunkel vor Nässe.

"That's all you have?" he asked, looking at the torn, black T-shirt I still had on. It was also wet and clung to my shoulders. "You're so thin. Wait here. I'll be right back." He left again, then returned with a white T-shirt and the brown sweater. The T-shirt said *New York is Book Country* on the front.

"Why don't you put these on?" He handed them to me.

I took them and looked around.

"You need a place to change," he realized. "Okay, come with me." He led me between some tall bookshelves. "You can change here. No one will see. Promise me you'll throw that black T-shirt in the garbage."

He left me there. I looked around to make sure he wasn't hiding in the other rows watching, then I stripped off the black T-shirt and put on the white one. I didn't like the sweater. But it felt soft and warm so I put it on.

I came out from the bookshelves. The library man had laid out my sweatshirt over the radiator.

"I'll be right back," he said.

Once again I waited, listening to the steam radiators hiss and my stomach rumble. The man returned, drying his hands on some paper towels like he just washed them.

"Okay, let's make a place for you," he said, carrying one of

3 **I'll be right back:** Ich bin gleich zurück. 9 **to change** (clothes)**:** sich umziehen. 14 **to hide:** (sich) verstecken. 21 **to rumble:** knurren.

the shopping bags over to a small round table. He put out a red plastic plate and a plastic cup, which he filled with Hawaiian Punch. On the plate he put one chocolate, one sugar, and one cinnamon donut.

"If you want anything more to eat or drink, I'll be over in the children's section." He pointed toward the side of the library where there were smaller tables and chairs and colorful posters on the walls. He picked up the shopping bags and left.

I ate the donuts and drank the punch in no time, but didn't ask for more right away. I was afraid he might say that I should leave. I wanted to get warm first. With food in my stomach I got warm faster. I watched the library man spread red tablecloths on the little tables in the children's room and then put out plates and cups. Now and then he looked in my direction and smiled.

Finally, I picked up my plate and cup and went over to him. The library man was putting books on the tables. Most of them showed a round-faced black man on the cover.

"Who's that?" I asked.

"Martin Luther King," the library man answered. "A very good man who made a difference for many people."

I held up my empty plate and cup.

3 **Hawaiian Punch:** Fruchtsaftgetränk. 4 **cinnamon:** Zimt. 22 **to make a difference for:** etwas bewirken für.

"I thought you might still be hungry." He filled my cup again and gave me three more donuts. I went back to the table at the front of the library and ate them. No one would ever write books about me. I would never make a difference to anyone.

Outside cars, trucks, and buses started going up and down the streets, their windshield wipers swiping back and forth. The snow was still coming down in big white clumps, but the streets slowly turned into gray slush. The same with the sidewalks where more and more people were now walking.

I sat at the small round table and watched through the big windows. It felt good to be in a warm place.

After a while the library man came over. "Still hungry?" he asked.

I shook my head.

"I want you to know that Bobby will be coming in soon. If you want to stay I promise that he won't hurt you. You have as much right to use this library as anyone else."

"I think I'll go. Thanks for the donuts." I got up and started to take off the brown sweater.

"No, I want you to keep it," he said.

"Okay, thanks." I took my sweatshirt from the radiator. The cuffs were frayed and it had holes in it, but it was only

9 **slush:** Matsch. 18 **to have the right to do s.th.:** ein Anrecht haben etw. zu tun. 23 **cuff:** Manschette, Ende eines Ärmels. **frayed:** ausgefranst.

damp now and even the dampness felt warm. I pulled it over my head. The library man looked outside at the falling snow. The lines in his blotchy freckled forehead deepened slightly. "Do you have somewhere to go?"

"Sure," I said, and started toward the doors. He walked with me. I pulled the doors open. The air smelled cold and fresh.

"Wait," he said. "My name is Anthony. Come back here any time you want. If you don't see me by the computer tables you can go to the front desk and ask for me. They'll get me, okay?"

"Okay." I left.

3 **freckled:** sommersprossig. **forehead:** Stirn.

THIRTEEN

By the time I got to the empty building, I was wet and shivering again. Pest barked when I came up the steps, but everyone else was fast asleep on the mattress or the floor, covered with blankets, discarded clothes, and rags. I looked around for Rainbow, but she wasn't there. I pulled together a bunch of clothes – pants, shirts, sweatshirts – and made a nest on the mattress and crawled into it. I'd been up most of the night looking for Rainbow and was quite worried. Now that I had those donuts in my stomach, it was easy to fall asleep.

"Maybe, wake up." Someone touched my shoulder. I opened my eyes. My breath was a white cloud in the dim room. I couldn't stop shaking and had to clench my teeth to stop them from chattering.

It was Tears who woke me. "2Moro got us free passes to *The Cradle* tonight."

11 **discarded:** ausrangiert. 14 **to crawl:** kriechen, krabbeln. 19 **dim:** schummrig. 22 **free pass:** Freikarte.

"How?" I yawned. *The Cradle* was the hottest club in the world and impossible to get into.

Tears looked over at 2Moro, who was kneeling in front of the broken mirror, putting makeup on Jewel, who was wearing a pink wig. "How'd you get the passes?"

"The bartender likes me," 2Moro said.

I sat up. My head was spinning and I felt dizzy. My ankles started to itch something fierce and I had to scratch them hard. It was the bedbugs. Even the frigid cold didn't stop them.

"I'm not going to some club," I said.

Maggot was reading a newspaper. "Here's something that might change your mind. The weather forecast is for record lows tonight. Like in the teens."

"You sure that's today's paper?" OG asked.

Maggot turned it around and looked at the front page. "Yeah. And with the wind chill it's supposed to feel even colder."

I scratched my ankles so hard my fingernails broke the skin and my fingertips became damp and sticky with blood. But the pain made the horrible itching easier to take. Pushing myself up to my feet, I found that when I stood I was dizzy. The thin shafts of light squeezing past the window frames

5 **wig:** Perücke. 6 **bartender:** Barkeeper. 7 **my head was spinning:** in meinen Kopf drehte sich alles. **dizzy:** schwindlig. **ankle:** Knöchel. 8 **to itch something fierce:** total jucken. 9 **bedbug:** Wanze. **frigid:** eisig. 17 **wind chill:** durch den Wind verursachte Kälte. 23 **shaft of light:** Lichtstrahl. **window frame:** Fensterrahmen.

cut through the dim room like sabers. Dust floated in the shafts and shimmered. All the different tiny shapes catching the sunlight and turning white like snowflakes. When I breathed out, the cloud of my breath mixed with them and made them swirl and dance.

"Now do you want to go?" Tears asked me.

I looked at Maggot. "Are you going?"

"Oh, yeah." He grinned devilishly. "I sold all those roofies there. They all think I've got really good stuff. This time I'll sell a couple of spoonfuls of baking soda for hundreds of bucks."

"Can I go?" Tears asked.

OG was feeding Pest leftover noodles. "Hell, yes. They like 'em young in the clubs. Younger the better."

Tears bit her lip nervously.

"Not to worry, sweetheart," Jewel told her. "We'll make you look twenty-one."

"What'll we wear?" I asked. All I had was my sweatshirt and the white T-shirt and brown sweater Anthony gave me. Tears was wearing a furry black and orange sweater that made her look like one of those caterpillars you sometimes saw on roads.

"I can get you clothes, too," said 2Moro.

1 **saber:** Säbel. **to float:** schweben. 8 **devilish:** teuflisch. 10 **baking soda:** Backpulver. 13 **leftover:** übrig geblieben. 21 **caterpillar:** Raupe.

Everyone except OG went. He was too old and crusty. With that beard and hair and missing teeth he could never get into the club no matter who 2Moro knew.

It was dark when we left the building. Outside the snow and slush had turned hard and icy. I kept slipping on the sidewalk. Jewel had such a hard time walking in his platform shoes that he needed 2Moro and me to hold his arms so he didn't fall.

2Moro led us to a building on Avenue A. It was five stories tall and made of brick. A rusty fire escape zigzagged down the front. The front door was unlocked and the mailboxes in the hallway were dented and broken. Light came from a bare light bulb hanging by a wire from the ceiling.

"My, how luxurious," Jewel said.

2Moro led us up the stairs. On the second flight a group of Goths were coming down. They had dyed black hair and black eye makeup and lipstick and nail polish and were wearing black leather coats and high lace-up black boots.

"Looks like the cold forced the street scum inside," the lead Goth snickered when he saw us. A wooden cross hung from his left ear.

"Welcome to the young bourgeois! If it isn't the bridge and tunnel crowd," Maggot shot back. "How's life in the sub-

6 **platform shoes:** Plateauschuhe. 9 **five stories tall:** fünf Stockwerke hoch. 10 **fire escape:** Feuerleiter. **to zigzag down:** im Zickzack herunterführen. 11 **mailbox:** Briefkasten. 12 **dented:** verbeult. 15 **flight:** Treppe. 22 **bourgeois:** Bourgeois; Spießbürger.

urbs, kids? Where'd you stash your regular clothes? In a locker at the train station?"

"Drop dead," the lead Goth snarled. "Anybody can be a bum. It don't prove nothing."

I thought there might be a fight, but we passed each other without another word. From the floor above came voices and thumping music. The air started to smell sweet and smoky.

"Is this the club?" Tears asked.

"Oh, no, my dear," Jewel answered. "This is just the warm up."

2Moro led us into the apartment. It was filled with smoke and kids. Most of them dressed in fashionable clean clothes. In the living room people were draped over the couches and chairs, or sitting on the floor watching a DVD of one of the *Lord of the Rings* movies. The air was so smoky it was hard to breathe. A kid with white-rimmed nostrils staggered up to Maggot. "Hey, you got anything?"

"Not for you," Maggot answered and turned away.

Tears stretched up and pressed her lips close to 2Moro's ear. "I thought he was going to sell baking powder."

"Not here," 2Moro whispered back. "Too easy to get caught."

1 **to stash:** bunkern. 2 **locker:** Gepäckfach. 4 **bum:** Penner. 10 **warm up:** Aufwärmrunde. 14 **to be draped over:** sich lümmeln auf. 17 **white-rimmed nostrils:** Nasenlöcher mit weißem Rand (vom Kokainschnupfen). 22 **to get caught:** geschnappt werden.

2Moro took Tears and me by the hand. "Come on, let's see what we can find you to wear." She led us down a narrow hallway. It seemed like every room was filled with people.

"What are they all doing here?" Tears asked.

"Waiting," 2Moro said. "It's not cool to get to the club before midnight."

She led us into a bedroom where some kids were sitting around, drinking beer and smoking. Someone was in the bed, sleeping with earplugs and a black mask over his eyes. One of the smoking kids raised a finger to his lips, warning us to be quiet.

"Over here," 2Moro whispered, pulling open a closet door. The closet was stuffed with silk shirts, tank tops and black slacks. The floor was covered with shoes.

"Whose clothes is this?" I whispered to 2Moro.

"That bartender I told you about," she answered. "His girlfriend works in a clothing store."

"He has a girlfriend?" Tears asked. "I thought he liked you."

2Moro shrugged. "Come on, we'll get you dressed."

It didn't take long for Tears and me to find clothes that fit. Some of them still had sales tags attached. The bathroom was crowded with kids, but we managed to squeeze in and

3 **hallway:** Gang. 9 **earplug:** Ohrstöpsel. 12 **closet:** Wandschrank. 14 **covered:** bedeckt. 21 **to fit:** passen. 22 **sales tag:** Preisschild. **attached:** angeheftet.

wash our hands and faces. Then 2Moro started to make us up.

"Ow!" I yelped in pain when she tried to pull a plastic brush through my hair. "Stop! It hurts."

"You can't go to the club like this," 2Moro said. "Your hair's disgusting. We have to do something with it."

"Well, not that," I said.

"Okay, let me try this," she said. Working more gently, she managed to free enough hair to cover the hopelessly matted, tangled parts. Then she used mousse to make it stiff so it would stay in place. "You can fake it for tonight, but you ever want to do something with this mess, all the detangler in the world ain't gonna help. This is hopeless, girl. You got to cut it all off and start over."

"Maybe," I said.

2Moro moved over to Tears, whose hair was short and not so tangled.

Looking at myself in the mirror, with my face washed and my hair brushed and those new clothes, I began to feel excited about going to *The Cradle*. We left the bathroom and met Maggot and Jewel near the front door. A lot of people had left their coats in the hall. Maggot picked one out and handed it to me. "This looks like it'll fit."

9 **matted:** verfilzt. 10 **tangled:** verwirrt, verheddert. 11 **to fake s.th.:** etw. vortäuschen. **mousse:** Schaumfestiger. 19 **to feel excited:** aufgeregt sein. 23 **to hand s.th. to s.o.:** jdm. etwas geben.

"But it's not mine," I said.

"These are rich kids," Maggot said. "They lose a jacket, their parents'll buy them a new one."

With new clothes and warm jackets we left the apartment and went back down to the street. The cold stung my nose and ears, and I hugged my new coat tightly around me and wished I'd taken a hat and gloves, too. Our breath came out in long white streams of mist.

The Cradle wasn't far away. A long line of people stood outside in the bitter cold. Everyone was made up. Wigs and feathers and fingernails in every possible color. Shoes and boots with heels that added six inches. I felt good being in a crowd like that. Hardly anyone stared at me. 2Moro led us toward the front of the line, but we could hardly go more than a few feet without someone stopping Maggot.

"Hey, Mag, you got any roofies?"

"What you got, Mag?"

"Hey, roofie boy, you got any?"

"Inside," Maggot answered every time. "Inside."

We got to the front of the line. A big guy wearing a huge brown fur coat and a fuzzy black hat was blocking the door. He raised a hand the size of a bear's paw. "Far as you go."

2Moro reached into her little black handbag and pulled out

5 **to sting, stung, stung:** stechen. 8 **stream of mist:** feuchter Dunst. 12 **heel:** Absatz. 21 **fur coat:** Pelzmantel. 22 **paw:** Tatze. **far as you go:** bis hierhin und nicht weiter.

some orange slips of paper. The furry bear studied them, then nodded. "Okay, the five of you, go in."

He pulled open the door and a gust of music, flashing lights, and hot smoky air blew into our faces. A moment later we were inside and the door banged closed behind us. At first the music was too loud, the flashing lights blinding, and the smoke even thicker than in the apartment. But we got used to it. Maggot was surrounded by people asking what he had and how much he wanted. Jewel and 2Moro disappeared into the dancing crowd. I felt a hand close around mine and squeeze tightly. It was Tears.

"You ever been to a club before?" I asked.

She shook her head.

"You know how Jewel and 2Moro sometimes disappear for days?" I said. "This is where they go."

"How do they eat and sleep?" Tears asked.

"Other people have money. Sometimes a lot of it. They pay $8 for a bottle of beer and $25 for a little pizza."

"What about sleep?" Tears asked.

"Sometimes they don't," I said. "Sometimes they nap in the clubs. Or people who let them live in their apartments for a while."

"For free?"

3 **gust:** Stoß, Schwall. 6 **blinding:** blendend. 8 **surrounded by:** umgeben von. 20 **to nap:** ein Nickerchen machen. 23 **for free:** umsonst.

"Sometimes."

I wasn't sure Tears heard my answer. She started bouncing to the music. "Want to dance?"

"Okay."

We moved into the crowd and started to dance. Like a little kid at the zoo, Tears kept looking at all the exotic creatures around us, but she stayed close to me. A man started to dance with us. He was probably around 40 and wore a shiny black shirt and a gold chain. His shirt was open and we could see his curly black chest hair. On one wrist was a gold watch and on the other a gold bracelet, and he wore three gold rings.

"Haven't seen you two around here before," he said over the music.

Tears and I kept dancing.

"Pretty hot in here," he said. "Want something to drink?"

I felt terribly thirsty, and my throat was dry from the smoke. The guy waved us over. "Come on, I'll buy you both a drink," he said.

I figured as long as Tears and I stuck together we were safe. We followed him away from the dancing floor to a long bar. Except for the glow of cigarette embers and the ghostly outline of the bartender's white shirt, it was almost completely dark.

2 **to bounce:** hüpfen. 9 **chain:** Kette. 10 **chest:** Brust. 11 **bracelet:** Armband. 18 **the guy waved us over:** der Typ winkte uns heran. 20 **to figure:** sich etw. denken. 22 **ghostly outline:** geisterhafter Umriss.

"I'm Jack," the guy said and sat on one of the bar stools. "First time here?"

We both nodded.

"What'll you have?"

We both ordered Cokes. Jack took out a pack of cigarettes and offered us some. Better not, I thought, and shook my head.

"It's a good place," Jack said. "People don't hassle you. You hear what they have to offer. You don't like it, you move on. Know what I mean?"

I nodded. Tears didn't. The bartender came back with two glasses filled with brown liquid. Jack took a thick bunch of bills from his pocket and paid. Each drink had a thin red straw. I sipped mine. It tasted funny, but not bad, and it was cold and refreshing. Next to me, Tears didn't seem to mind the taste of her drink, either.

"Wow," said Jack. "You two really were thirsty." He motioned to the bartender for two more. The bartender slid new glasses across the bar to us and Tears and I both started to sip through the thin red straws. Out of the corner of my eye I thought I saw a familiar-looking head of blond hair in the dancing crowd. Could it be Rainbow?

"Hey, where're you going?" Jack asked.

1 **bar stool:** Barhocker. 8 **to hassle:** belästigen, bedrängen. 12 **liqid:** Flüssigkeit. **bunch of bills:** Bündel Geldscheine. 14 **to sip:** nippen an. 17 **to motion:** ein Zeichen geben. 21 **familiar-looking:** vertraut aussehend.

"Be right back," I said and gave Tears a look that said: "Don't go nowhere." She winked and sipped her drink.

I only had to take one step to know that whatever made the Coke taste funny also made me feel funny. I stumbled and almost lost my balance. But it wasn't a bad feeling. I felt giddy and bold. I went right to the dance floor and stepped into the crowd of warm, sweaty, moving bodies. I bumped into a few dancers, but no one seemed to care. Some even waved to me to join them.

It was tempting to stop and dance. Whatever was in that drink seemed to open a door inside me that welcomed the beat and rhythm of the music. And anyway, there was no sign of Rainbow on the dance floor. Thanks to the drink and the darkness and the swirling bodies and the flashing lights, I was sure I only imagined her.

I began to dance. If the other dancers saw me, they smiled. I felt like they liked me. No one seemed to care about my skin condition. Before, when I danced with Tears, I felt like I was dancing only with her. But now I felt like I was dancing with everyone. It felt good. The music. The movement. You could lose yourself here. Forget all about the rest of your life. Forget that your ankles itched and your stomach hurt, forget you were sick. Or hungry. Or lonely.

2 **to wink:** zwinkern. 6 **giddy:** schwindlig; auf eine leichtfertige Art sorglos. **bold:** kühn. 7 **to bump into:** zusammenstoßen mit. 14 **swirling:** wirbelnd. 15 **to imagine:** sich etw. einbilden.

When I did see Rainbow, I thought I was imagining it again. But I looked more closely and knew it was her. She was dancing with someone, only not really dancing. Her face was buried in his shoulder and her arms were wrapped around his neck, hanging on like she'd fall if she let go. On her right wrist were two plastic tags. One was white and the other blue.

The man she was dancing with turned her around. So now I could see him. He was old. Older than Jack. He was mostly bald on top, and the short hair around the sides of his head was gray. His face was heavy and lined.

My heart started to race with happiness and I pushed through the crowd toward them. "Rainbow!"

She lifted her head and rested her chin on the man's shoulder. Most of the scabs on her face had healed and the new skin was pink. Her eyes opened slowly. Even though she was only a few feet away, it seemed to take her a long time to focus on me. "Hi." She smiled sweetly, but her voice sounded syrupy.

"You okay?" I asked.

Before Rainbow could answer, the man turned around. His jaw was covered with dark stubble. He had a thin moustache and small, dark eyes. "What do you want?"

4 **to wrap around:** umschlingen. 6 **tag:** Schildchen, Etikett. 11 **lined:** faltig. 19 **syrupy:** klebrig. 22 **stubble:** Bartstoppeln. **moustache:** Schnurrbart.

"She's my friend," I said. "I ain't seen her in a while."

"She's busy," the man said.

"I just wanted to say hi."

"Another time."

"You don't have to be so mean."

I don't know why I said that. Maybe it was the drinks Jack gave me. Maybe I just didn't like the way this man was holding Rainbow so close.

"Get lost," the man said.

"Screw you."

A hand closed around my arm and pulled so hard my feet left the floor. The grip was like a steel clamp and I couldn't shake it off. I was half-dragged through the crowd, but I couldn't see who was pulling me. Just a big hand with black hairs on the back and a thick gold double ring around the third and fourth fingers. We left the dance floor and the hand spun me around and shoved me. My ribs hit the hard edge of the bar, and I lost my breath. The hand grabbed my arm again and squeezed painfully. Now I could see who grabbed me. The guy was short and was wearing a tight white T-shirt. His arms and neck were thick and muscular. His face was square and his head was shaved. His scalp glis-

10 **screw you:** fick dich. 12 **steel clamp:** Schraubzwinge aus Stahl. 13 **to shake s.th. off:** etw. abschütteln. 18 **edge:** Kante. 19 **to squeeze:** (zu)drücken. 22 **to glisten:** glänzen.

tened under the lights. He had diamond earrings in both ears.

"Let go." I tried to break free. Another hand came out of nowhere and slapped me hard in the face. It stung and made me feel dizzy. When I opened my eyes, I saw a bartender in a white shirt down at the end of the bar, watching.

"What your problem?" the short man with the shaved head asked. He spoke with an accent.

"I want to talk to my friend."

"She not your friend," the man said.

"Yes, she is."

"She belong to me," said the man. "She only do what I tell her. She only talk to who I tell her."

"Who are you?" I asked.

"Not your problem," he said.

He was still squeezing my arm. I didn't try to fight. I didn't want him to hit me again. "Let me go, *please*."

"The girl belongs to me." He squeezed my arm harder.

"Okay, okay. Just let go."

He let go. I looked back at the dancers. Rainbow's arms were still around the older man's neck. Once again her face was buried in his shoulder.

I walked back to the place where I left Tears and Jack, but they weren't there. I looked for them, and for Maggot or

4 **to slap s.o. in the face:** jnd. ohrfeigen.

2Moro, who might know where they went. All I saw was Jewel dancing and Rainbow hanging onto the older man. All of a sudden I felt terribly tired. I found stairs that led up to a balcony. There were padded booths and tables up there. It was very dark. I could hear people whispering and giggling. I found an empty booth and lay down.

"Hey, get up."

Something scratchy brushed against my arm and I opened my eyes. The lights were on and I squinted. A tall thin guy was standing next to the booth, holding a broom.

"Time to go," he said. He was the bartender who watched while the man with the shaved head hurt me.

"I don't got nowhere to go," I said with a yawn.

"I am sorry, but you gotta leave," he said. "We're closing."

I sat up, feeling dizzy. Things inside my head were spinning. "Okay, give me a second."

The bartender started sweeping the floor. I sat in the booth and waited for my head to stop swirling. After a while he glanced at me and I knew I had to go. I stood up, but my head began to spin again and my stomach felt queasy. I sat down, waited a few seconds, then tried again. This time the spinning and queasiness weren't as bad.

I took the stairs down. With the lights on, the club looked

4 **padded:** gepolstert. **booth:** Sitzbank. 8 **scratchy:** kratzend. **to brush against:** streifen. 9 **to squint:** die Augen zusammenkneifen; schielen. 13 **yawn:** Gähnen. 20 **my stomach felt queasy:** mir war etwas übel.

different. The seats in the booths were patched with strips of black tape. Over the dance floor rows of spotlights hung from black metal racks. Above the lights the ceiling was a shadowy patchwork of different colors and peeling flakes of paint. The whole place looked like it was thrown together in an afternoon.

I heard voices from downstairs. The last of the partiers were filing out the door into the cold dark. One of them was wearing a pink wig. It was Jewel.

"Hey," I called out.

Jewel turned. "Maybe? Come on, we're going to *Stanley's*."

I didn't know what *Stanley's* was and I didn't care, as long as there was a chance I could lie down again and sleep.

1 **patched with strips of black tape:** mit schwarzem Klebeband geflickt.

FOURTEEN

It was so cold I started to shiver the moment I stepped outside. We hurried down the icy sidewalk. Someone said *Stanley's* was an after-hours place. We went around a corner and down some steps, and Jewel rapped his knuckles against a red metal door. A slot in the door slid open and a pair of eyes looked out.

"*Stanley's* so cool," Jewel said to the eyes. It must have been a password because I heard the metal clacks of locks being undone, and then the door was opened by a fat man wearing a black shirt. Behind him was a dark basement with music and some sofas and a small bar.

"Twenty bucks," the man said.

Some of the people who came with us from *The Cradle* paid him and went in. Then only Jewel and I were left outside.

"I don't have twenty dollars," Jewel said.

The fat man pointed back into the basement. "You see the

10 **after-hours place:** Laden, der die ganze Nacht über geöffnet bleibt. 11 **to rap one's knuckles:** mit den Knöcheln klopfen. 12 **slot:** Schlitz. 16 **to undo:** aufmachen. 23 **to point:** deuten.

guy with the short brown hair sitting on the couch? I think he'll like you. Go see if you can get him to buy you a few drinks."

"My pleasure." Jewel went in.

The fat man stared at me. "You don't have no money, either?"

I shook my head. The man started to close the door.

"Wait," I said. "It's freezing and I'm really tired."

"This ain't no homeless shelter."

"Please?"

The man sighed. "Look, kid, no offense or nothing, but if you want to glom around places like this you gotta have something to offer. Looks or drugs or something."

"I could work."

The man pressed his lips together and scratched his head. "You know how to wash dishes?"

I nodded.

"My dishwasher's broken. Go back in the kitchen and wash all the dishes in the sink and on the counter. Then find yourself a place to sleep."

The kitchen was through a door behind the basement. It was tiny and narrow and lit by a bare light bulb hanging from the ceiling. If the dirty dishes in the sink and on the

4 **my pleasure:** gern geschehen; mit Vergnügen. 10 **homeless shelter:** Heim für Obdachlose. 11 **no offense or nothing:** nimm's mir nicht übel. 12 **to glom around:** sich herumtreiben. 13 **looks:** gutes Aussehen. 18 **dishwasher:** Geschirrspüler. 19 **sink:** Spüle. **counter:** Küchenzeile. 22 **bare light bulb:** nackte Glühbirne.

counter were piled any higher, they would have slid off and smashed on the floor.

Washing the dishes and getting my hands wet woke me up for a while. The fat man came in twice. Once to make sure I was working. And a second time to make some hot dogs in the microwave. Cigarette smoke hung in the air, and I could hear laughter and talking from the other room. Finally, when I couldn't keep my eyes open no longer, I rolled a smelly kitchen towel into a pillow and went to sleep under the table.

When I woke up, I could see a pair of wide pink feet in green rubber flip-flops. They belonged to the fat man. He was standing at the sink. I crawled out from under the table. The air was warm and steamy. A big pot of spaghetti was boiling on the stove.

"You got a bathroom?"

"Through that door." The fat man pointed.

I used the bathroom and came back out.

"You did good work, kid. You can finish doing the dishes," the fat man said. "Then clean up the rest of the kitchen and the bathroom. Help yourself to whatever's in the refrigerator. Stay as long as you want."

He finished making the spaghetti and left. I looked in the

1 **to pile:** stapeln. 2 **to smash:** zerbrechen. 4 **to make sure:** sich versichern. 9 **pillow:** Kissen.

refrigerator. It was almost empty, but I found an open container of yogurt. After I skimmed the fuzzy green stuff off the surface, the yogurt underneath wasn't bad. Then I found some stale bread and made it into toast. There was even some chocolate ice cream in the freezer.

After I ate, I finished cleaning the kitchen. The bathtub in the bathroom was square and half the size of a regular tub. I decided I wanted to take a bath, but the brown ring around the tub was thick and gummy. I was kneeling next to the tub, scrubbing it with scouring powder, when the bathroom door opened. A girl with lots of piercings and bright orange hair came in and sat down on the toilet. She was smoking a cigarette and muttering to herself. I don't think she even noticed me.

When I finished cleaning the bathtub I took a bath. Even though the tub was only big enough for me to sit, the hot water felt good around my legs and hips. I scooped it up in my hands and splashed it on my head and felt the water run down my back and arms. I closed my eyes and remembered when I was little, sitting in the old metal washtub in the trailer kitchen, my mom pouring hot water on my shoulders from a pitcher, then washing my back with a washcloth. Her soft, soothing voice. The perfumed smell of the soap.

2 **to skim off:** abschöpfen. **fuzzy:** pelzig. 3 **surface:** Oberfläche. 4 **stale:** alt. 6 **bathtub:** Badewanne. 10 **to scrub:** schrubben. **scouring powder:** Scheuerpulver. 14 **to notice:** bemerken. 21 **trailer:** Wohnwagen. 22 **pitcher:** Krug.

The toy boat and the little black-and-white windup orca that would slap its tail and bump its nose against the sides of the tub.

Sometimes I would ask my mom about my dad, but she always said he was just someone she knew and it didn't matter because we had each other and we were all we needed. But then another man started to come around and I didn't see much of my mom. And then I had a little sister. And that was the way it went. There'd be a man around for a while, and then there'd be a new baby. And there were no more baths. Only trailers with showers sometimes. And always tons of laundry to do. Heaps of baby clothes and sheets and towels and blankets that smelled of pee. And dishes to wash and baby bottles to clean and bathrooms to scrub.

At night Mom would stumble in slurring her words and smelling like smoke, saying I was worthless and stupid and ugly and she wished she never had me. And then there'd be the stinging slap of a leather belt against the backs of my legs, or a pinch so hard it drew blood, and once, a burning-hot iron.

Even then I stayed, like Tears, not knowing what else to do. But then, about a week after the iron, she hit me with a lamp and opened up my head. She told the nurse at the hospital

1 **windup orca:** aufziehbarer (Spielzeug-)Killerwal. 12 **laundry:** Wäsche. 13 **pee:** Pisse. 15 **to slur:** undeutlich sprechen. 18 **to sting:** brennen. **slap:** Schlag. 19 **pinch:** Kneifen.

that I fell down, but they took me to another room and asked if that was true and I said no. I told the nurse what really happened, and after they stitched my head they put me in a home with other kids, and the next time I saw my mom she said she hated me and never wanted to see me again.

Now, sitting in the bathtub, I cupped my hands together and raised some water over my head. But the water was only lukewarm and it made me shudder immediately. I got out of the tub and realized that there were no towels. So I just stood there waiting and trembling. And when I was only damp I pulled on my new party clothes again and went back into the kitchen.

I was sitting at the table when the fat guy came in. "You still here?" He really seemed surprised. I had a feeling he forgot about me. He looked in the bathroom. "Hey, nice job, thanks. Why don't you come back again next week?"

"I can't stay?" I asked.

"You kidding?" he said. "It's bad enough I'm running an after-hours club. The cops come in and find a minor here, I'll go to jail."

"But you said if I cleaned up I could stay as long as I wanted."

3 **to stitch:** nähen. 10 **to realize:** bemerken. 19 **you kidding?:** Machst du Witze? 20 **minor:** Minderjährige(r). 21 **jail:** Gefängnis.

"You musta heard me wrong, kid. I said you could stay as long as you worked. No work, no stay. Like I said, come back in a week. I'll have more for you to do by then."

He was lying. Another grown-up who used kids to get what they wanted. But there was nothing I could do, so I left and went outside.

It was daylight. Morning. People carried paper cups of coffee and newspapers on their way to work. Their coats were partly unbuttoned, their scarves hung loose, and their gloves stuck out of pockets. It was warmer again.

Sometimes I like to walk. Even if I don't know where I was going. Just got to a corner and went the way that felt best. Or if I been to that corner already, I went the other way. Then I stopped at a corner and didn't go nowhere. People gave me looks. Nothing made you stranger in the city than not going nowhere. Standing still meant you either had nowhere to go or you had somewhere to go and you didn't want to go there. Maybe other people felt that way and just didn't want to admit it. Everybody acted like they had somewhere to go. But why did everyone always have to have somewhere to go? Why did they have to do what everyone else did? Why did they think you were weird if you did something different? Maggot called them robots because

4 **to lie:** lügen. 9 **unbuttoned:** nicht zugeknöpft. 15 **strange:** fremd. 19 **to admit:** zugeben. 22 **weird:** seltsam, merkwürdig.

they all got up in the morning and ate the same things for breakfast, then went off and did the same work all day, then came home and ate the same things for dinner and went to sleep. Why didn't it bother them? Or maybe the question was, why did it bother us?

I was walking along the sidewalk when I saw Jewel sitting at a table by the window in a coffee shop, his chin propped in his hand. He was wearing a bulky olive-colored coat and his hair was in cornrows. He was staring down at the little table like he was all partied out forever.

I tapped on the window. He raised his head and looked at me. The blank expression didn't change. He put both hands on the table and pushed slowly, like he needed all his strength to get up.

He came out of the coffee shop carrying his pink wig and other clothes in a wrinkled brown *Macy's* paper bag. His eyes were still made up, but they were also red. His skin had a greenish tint, his jaw was lined with dark stubble. Looked like he hadn't slept in days.

"You okay?" I asked.

"What's okay?" he said.

"I'm going back," I said. "You want to come?"

"Why not?" he said like he didn't care.

4 **to bother:** stören. 9 **in cornrows:** Frisur, bei der das Haar zu vielen dünnen Zöpfen geflochten wird. 12 **blank expression:** leerer Gesichtsausdruck. 16 **wrinkled:** zerknittert.

We went to a bus stop. A lot of people were waiting to take the bus to work. They were wearing clean clothes and had freshly washed faces and neat hair. Most of them carried briefcases.

A bus came. Jewel and I snuck on through the back doors where people usually got off. Inside, I looked toward the front. The driver was watching us in the rearview mirror. A second later the engine roared and the bus pulled away from the curb. The seats were all taken, so Jewel and me had to stand and hold onto a pole.

The people on the bus stared at us. Jewel and I traded glances, like trying to tell each other that they were the strange ones, not us. But I looked in the bus window and saw our reflections. Two ragged, scrawny kids and a wrinkled brown paper bag with a bright pink wig sticking partway out of it.

Who really were the strange ones?

The bus stopped and some people got up from their seats. Jewel and I sat down. I heard a sob. Jewel was pressing his face into his hands. The people sitting across from us were watching him.

"What's wrong?" I whispered.

Jewel sobbed and choked a little. He moaned sorrowfully,

5 **to sneak, snuck, snuck:** sich schleichen. 7 **rearview mirror:** Rückspiegel. 10 **pole:** Haltestange. 11 **to trade glances:** Blicke tauschen. 14 **ragged:** zerlumpt, abgerissen. **scrawny:** dürr. 19 **sob:** Schluchzer.

then coughed and sniffed and sobbed again as if a bolt of new agony had just surged through him. But it was not, I thought, physical pain that he felt. It was a different pain. The pain of this cold, hungry, dirty life where nobody cared whether you lived or died. Where you were not even a name. Not even a number. Just some flesh clinging to some bones. Waiting to be fed or not be fed. To sleep or not sleep. To live or not live no more.

"What's wrong, Jewel?" I asked again.

"They don't want me anymore," Jewel sobbed.

"Who?"

He raised his head from his hands. His eyes were red and his cheeks were streaked with tears and make-up. "The ones who pay for everything. They say I'm too old. Once you start to shave, once you get some hair on your chest, they don't want you anymore. What am I going to do?"

"Go home."

Jewel blinked and fresh tears ran out of his eyes and down his cheeks. "Real home? I can't. My father hates me. My mother says she loves me but that I'm sick and I need help. I don't need help. I just need someone who'll love and take care of me."

Dream on, I thought.

2 **agony:** Qual. **to surge:** branden; schießen. 3 **physical pain:** körperlicher Schmerz.

"Where's 2Moro?" I asked.

"Who knows? She's a pretty girl. There'll always be men who'll want her." Jewel wiped his eyes with the sleeve of the coat, smearing the remaining mascara. The bus stopped abruptly. We got off and walked along the sidewalk, past the *Good Life* and Piss Alley to the empty building. The black metal front door was open and construction workers wearing yellow hardhats were up on the scaffolding. Two workers came through the front door with the bedbug mattress and threw it into the Dumpster. On the second floor a woman wearing a blue hardhat came to the window and tipped a white plastic bucket into a wooden chute. Candles and makeup and clothes slid down the shoot and into the Dumpster.

We weren't living there no more.

We walked to the park. The trees were dark and bare. The gray squirrels wore thick winter coats. Maggot was sitting at one of the concrete tables playing chess with an old man with a white beard. He and the old man were bundled up in coats and hats and gloves.

"Maggot?" I said.

"Hold on," he said and stared at the chess pieces for a long time. We waited. Maggot moved a piece. The old man

4 **mascara:** Wimperntusche. 7 **construction worker:** Bauarbeiter. 8 **hardhat:** Schutzhelm. **scaffolding:** Gerüst. 12 **chute:** Rutsche. 18 **chess:** Schach. 22 **hold on:** Warte.

frowned and swore under his breath. Maggot put on a broad grin and turned to Jewel and me.

"What's up?" he asked.

"Where'd everyone go?" Jewel asked.

"Under the bridge," Maggot said.

Jewel and me left the park. In the distance we could see Brooklyn Bridge, rising up from the streets below. Gray icicles hung from the sides, and the bridge got taller and taller until it was as high as a building. We could hear the roar of the cars racing above. The smell of exhaust was everywhere. A few blocks away, down where the bridge started to go over the river, a dull blue tarp was tied to the bridge wall. We kept walking until we got to a chain link fence. The blue tarp was on the other side. Jewel found a hole in the fence and we went through. A dog began to bark and OG pulled a corner of the tarp back and looked out at us.

"Lovely digs, OG," Jewel said.

Without a word, OG let the corner of the tarp fall. I bent down and crawled inside. It was like being in a tent. Somewhere OG found a small cooking stove. He had some plastic milk containers filled with water, some noodle packages, and some candles. Pest lay on his tummy and gnawed on a bone. Someone was curled up in a dirty, orange sleeping

1 **to swear under one's breath:** vor sich hinfluchen. 9 **roar:** Donnern, Tosen. 10 **exhaust:** Abgase. 12 **tarp** (tarpaulin): Plane. 13 **chain link fence:** Maschendrahtzaun. 17 **lovely digs:** nette Bude. 20 **cooking stove:** Herd. 22 **tummy:** Bauch. **to gnaw:** nagen.

bag. I looked closer and saw strands of blond hair over the collar of a black leather jacket. It was Rainbow!

Jewel crawled in and looked around with a sour expression. "Well, at least it's out of the rain and snow," he said.

I sat down near Rainbow and waited for her to wake up. Cars roared overhead. I could feel the vibrations through the bridge wall and listened to the endless whine of the engines and the horns and the occasional screech of tires. The smell of car exhaust was heavy in the air. The tarp was open on the side that faced the river, and seagulls swooped low over the greenish water. White waves broke against the bow of a tugboat with a tall red smokestack as it slowly pulled a barge.

Rainbow stirred. She opened her eyes and looked up at me. "Hey." She yawned.

"Hey." I felt a smile on my lips. I was so happy to see her.

She stretched. The blue and white tags were still on her wrists. "Where you been?"

"Hangin' out," I said. "How about you?"

She shrugged.

"What happened with that guy at the club?" I asked.

"Which one?" she asked.

7 **whine:** Heulen. 8 **occasional:** gelegentlich. **screech:** Kreischen. **tire:** Reifen. 10 **seagull:** Seemöwe. **to swoop:** einen Sturzflug machen. 12 **tugboat:** Schlepper. **smokestack:** Schornstein. 13 **barge:** Last-, Frachtkahn. 14 **to stir:** sich regen.

"The one with the shaved head who said you belonged to him."

Rainbow shook her head slowly. "He just wanted to sell me. I don't need that. If anyone's going to sell me, it's me."

"He let you go?"

"I left. What was he going to do? Tell me I couldn't?"

"Possible."

"I waited until he was asleep. Then, good-bye. It ain't like he'll be able to find me."

FIFTEEN

Angel Perez, aka 2Moro, *born in West New York, New Jersey. Mother died of AIDS, Angel age four. Father unknown. Lived with grandmother, later with aunt. Chronic sexual and physical abuse by aunt's boyfriend. Age 8, diagnosed with HIV illness. Frequently absent from school. Age 11, diagnosed as emotionally disturbed. Sent to foster care family. Remanded to juvenile correction facility. Age 12, released. Age 13–14, multiple arrests, loitering, prostitution, possession of narcotics, resisting arrest. Last known address, New York City. Dead at the age of 15. Cause of death: strangulation.*

That night an icy wind blew the tarp down. OG put it back up, but a few minutes later it fell down again. We crawled close together and pulled the tarp over us like an extra blanket. Under it we lay on sheets of cardboard, in nests of rags

11 **abuse:** Missbrauch. 13 **absent:** abwesend. 14 **disturbed:** gestört. **foster care family:** Pflegefamilie. **to remand:** überweisen. 15 **juvenile correction facility:** Besserungsanstalt für Jugendliche. 17 **narcotics:** Rauschmittel. 18 **strangulation:** Erwürgen.

and newspapers and plastic bags. I hid my face in the darkness of my cocoon to escape the bitter wind that blew dirt and newspapers in circles around us. Our faces and hands and hair were caked with soot and dirt.

The wind slowed to a breeze in the morning. I poked my head out from under my covers. Sometime during the night Maggot showed up and was now sharing the orange sleeping bag with Rainbow. They lay with their backs to each other. He was reading a newspaper. Jewel was nestled in a large pile of plastic bags and newspapers and rags.

I had my arms around Pest so that only his head stuck out. The little dog felt warm, and with his brown head so close, my nose was filled with his dog smell. Burning gurgles in my stomach reminded me that it was empty, but it was too cold to get up and go to the church for breakfast or beg for money.

Pest barked. I saw OG hurrying across the road during a break in the traffic. In one hand he carried a dirty green plastic pail with a squeegee sticking out of it. Pest squirmed out of my arms and ran toward him. OG had tied a rope around Pest's neck to keep him from running in front of the cars, but Pest was too young and dumb to understand. He ran until the rope got taut and snapped him back. Then he pulled at it, crying and barking.

2 **cocoon:** Kokon, Hülle. 4 **caked:** verkrustet. **soot:** Ruß. 5 **to poke one's head:** seinen Kopf herausstecken. 13 **gurgles:** Gluckern. 14 **to remind:** erinnern. 19 **squeegee:** Wischer. 23 **taut:** gespannt, straff. **to snap back:** zurückreißen.

OG dropped the bucket. It tipped over and the squeegee fell out, followed by a small puddle of brownish slush. “Hey, Pest.” He picked up his puppy and gave him a hug. Pest happily licked OG’s dirty face, his tail wagging like crazy.

Maggot looked up from the newspaper. “Get any money?”

OG shook his head. “Water started to freeze.”

“Anyone heard from 2Moro?” Jewel asked.

“Probably hooked up with a sugar daddy,” Rainbow said with a yawn.

“I heard a bunch of kids went down to *Mardi Gras*,” added OG. “Maybe she went, too.”

Jewel shook his head. “She would have told me.” He sat up in his jumble of rags and newspapers, his jaw covered with dark stubble, his cornrows loose and ratty, sprouting tufts of brown hair. He started to rock back and forth, staring at the greenish brown river. The rest of us stayed huddled in our nests.

No one did much of anything except try to stay warm. Maggot flattened out the crumpled sheets of newspaper that made up our bedding and read through them. After a while he tore off a corner of the newspaper and nudged Rainbow. She read it.

I heard Maggot whisper, “It’s her.”

8 **to hook up with s.o.:** sich mit jdn. treffen. **sugar daddy:** wohlhabender (älterer) Mann, der eine(n) junge(n) Frau oder Mann aushält. 10 **Mardi Gras:** Karneval in New Orleans. 14 **sprouting:** sprießend. **tuft:** Büschel. 15 **to rock back and forth:** vorwärts und rückwärts schaukeln (oder wippen). 21 **to nudge s.o.:** jnd. anstupsen.

"What's it say?" I asked softly.

Maggot and Rainbow traded a look. Maggot shrugged. Rainbow motioned for me to crawl close to her. She put her lips right next to my ear and read in a whisper: *"Teenage Girl's Body Found in Park. The body of an unidentified female teenager was found yesterday in a wooded area near the FDR Drive. A jogger reported the discovery to the police, who said the body was naked from the waist down and wearing a red-and-orange patchwork jacket."*

I twisted my head around until my eyes met Rainbow's. She pressed a finger to her cracked lips and pointed at Jewel, who sat rocking nearby. Then she started to read again, *"The cause of death could not be determined, although police said it appeared she had been strangled. The body was sent to the medical examiners. Police described the victim as Hispanic, between the ages of 14 and 18, medium height, slim, with short dyed red hair and a black tattoo around her neck."*

It had to be 2Moro. The jacket, the hair, the tattoo.

Rainbow nodded sadly like she agreed with what I was thinking. Maggot was already reading another page of newspaper. I looked at Jewel, rocking back and forth, muttering to himself. He seemed far away.

6 **wooded area:** Waldgebiet. 7 **FDR Drive:** Uferstraße am East River in Manhattan. 8 **waist:** Taille. 13 **to determine:** feststellen. 14 **strangled:** erwürgt.

"Don't say nothing," Rainbow whispered in my ear. "It's too late now."

The breeze blew a speck of grit into my eye, and I retreated into the darkness of my nest, blinking to make it go away. My stomach ached something awful. I thought about Tompkins Square Park and the little squirrel that kept climbing up the trees, crying so mournfully. I needed to do something to get my mind off my stomach so I started to tear the newspaper story about 2Moro into little pieces. Ripped off a little piece at a time and dropped it into a pile. Then the breeze came and swept the little pieces away. 2Moro blew away with the wind.

Minutes passed. Or maybe they were hours. Maggot smoked the butt of a cigarette someone flicked out of a car. Rainbow got up and went away, then came back again. The little pieces of 2Moro's newspaper story scattered in the breeze. Some got pushed toward the river, where the wind made ripples across the muddy green water.

Jewel pushed himself up. "I'm hungry. It's freezing. This place is so horrid. The absolute pits. How can any of you live here?"

No one answered. He was right. This was the worst place yet. Worse than the empty building. Worse than the park.

3 **speck of grit:** Staubkorn. 7 **mournfully** (adv.): traurig; kläglich. 9 **to rip:** zerreißen. 14 **butt:** Kippe. 16 **to scatter:** sich zerstreuen; verstreuen. **breeze:** Brise. 20 **the absolute pits:** das Letzte.

Worse than a hard kitchen floor. I closed my eyes and pretended I wasn't there. I was floating in the air like a particle of dust, invisible and unnoticed. Except when I passed through a bright shaft of light. Then I glowed before disappearing again.

"Aren't you hungry?" Jewel asked.

Everyone probably was. But hunger was just one more ugly sensation. Like shivering. And dizziness. And itching. And knowing you were nothing.

"And no one has any money?" Jewel sounded disgusted.

"Do you?" Maggot asked.

"No, but I know where to get some." Jewel bent his head down and started undoing the cornrows. He shook his brown hair out. It was kinky and ragged. "Rainbow, darling, would you make me up? *So that I can go to work?"*

Rainbow crawled out of the sleeping bag and made Jewel up. Only it was so cold her hands shook and the makeup wouldn't go on right. She tried to fix Jewel's mascara, eye shadow, add blush to his cheeks, and paint his lips red. Everything got smeared. But there was no mirror, so Jewel couldn't see. He rummaged through his wrinkled *Macy's* bag, yanking out clothes, pulling on stockings and a red short skirt and a pair of women's shoes with straps. Under

1 **to pretend:** so tun als ob. 3 **invisible:** unsichtbar. 8 **sensation:** Gefühl. 10 **disgusted:** angewidert. 14 **kinky:** verdreht. **ragged:** zottig. 21 **to rummage through:** herumwühlen in.

the stockings and short skirt his legs were long and thin. The shoes had thick heels and he walked heavily in them, clomping around like a horse pulling a wagon. He pulled on a short brown-and-white jacket, a patchwork of fake leather and fake fur. Sliding his slender hands behind his neck, he flipped the hair out over the shoulders of the fur jacket. Then spun around on the toes of the shoes.

"How do I look, Maybe?"

The make up was smudged and his clothes were wrinkled and frayed. Sometimes Jewel could look like a girl. But today he just looked like a fucked-up boy trying to be a girl. Or even worse, like a sad clown.

"Very pretty," I lied.

Jewel smiled. He had red lipstick on his teeth. But it would not matter.

"I'm on my way to a better life. Ta ta." He gaily swung his little black bag and headed across the street.

"Can't get there from here," OG muttered.

Rainbow crawled back into the sleeping bag with Maggot. OG coughed and spit up something red. Seagulls circled in the air above the dirty green river. A siren passed on the bridge overhead.

Later, Maggot asked, "Anybody hungry?"

4 **fake:** nachgemacht. 5 **to slide:** schieben, gleiten lassen. **slender:** schlank. 7 **to spin, spun, spun:** drehen. 9 **smudged:** verschmiert.

"Yeah." Rainbow started to get up, so I did too. OG didn't move. Maggot and Rainbow and me went across the street to the sidewalk.

"Spare a quarter? Some kind of change?" Maggot said to a man wearing a long gray coat. The man ignored him.

"Spare change?" Maggot asked a man with a beard wearing a puffy light blue down jacket. "We're hungry and cold." Ignored again.

"Spare change?" Maggot asked a woman wearing a long red coat. She hurried past.

"Forget this," Maggot said. "Let's look for the Hare Krishnas."

The Hare Krishnas sometimes came around handing out plastic bowls of bean soup, but it must have been too cold for them. The church van that gave out hot dogs wasn't around either.

"Guess it's time to Dumpster dive," Maggot said.

In an alley behind a pizza place, Maggot climbed into a dark green Dumpster. I heard a loud meow, and two scrawny cats shot out of the Dumpster and scampered away down the alley. Maggot climbed back out. In his hands were a bunch of pizza slices.

"Cool," he said. "Frozen pizza."

4 **spare a quarter?:** Hast du etwas Kleingeld übrig? (*quarter*: 25-Cent-Stück). **change:** Wechselgeld. 11 **Hare Krishnas:** hinduistische Sekte, deren Mitglieder manchmal singend durch Straßen ziehen. 17 **to Dumpster dive:** in den Container springen. 20 **to shoot, shot, shot:** schießen. **to scamper:** huschen.

The slices were hard as rock, but we broke off pieces and put them in our mouths and waited for them to soften. Eating pizza that way just made me feel colder, and before long I felt as chilled inside as I was outside.

"What a feast!" Maggot raved when we were done. "Who wants to go to the deli for coffee and dessert?"

I'd go anyplace that might be warm. On the way we met the boy named Lost, the one with the orange-tipped Mohawk. He was wearing a thick gray blanket around his shoulders like a shawl. He said something to Rainbow that I couldn't hear.

"See you guys later," Rainbow said and went off with him. I felt my heart ache.

"She's all you've got, huh?" Maggot's voice caught me by surprise. He was looking at me with a soft, sad expression on his face. He didn't say it in a mean way. Just pitying, which might have even been worse. I started to walk, staring down at the sidewalk.

Maggot caught up to me. "Hey, Maybe, I'm sorry."

"Don't be."

"It's just –" he started, then stopped, then started again. "It's just hard for me to believe that this is your whole life."

"It's your life, too," I reminded him.

"Yeah … I guess."

5 **What a feast!:** Was für ein Festmahl! **to rave:** schwärmen. 16 **to pity:** bemitleiden.

We begged outside the *Good Life* until someone bought us coffee.

Later on Rainbow came along dragging her feet, her eyes as blank as a zombie's. She backed against the wall and dropped down hard to the sidewalk, where she sat with her head nodding, blond hair hanging down between her knees.

4 **blank:** leer. **zombie:** Zombie, Untoter.

SIXTEEN

It was dark when the police van came around the corner. I was sitting against the wall next to Rainbow. The cops only used the van when they did a sweep. Most of the time we ran away. But Rainbow wasn't running nowhere.

The van stopped at the curb, and Officer Ryan got out. She was wearing white surgical gloves. I stood up on the sidewalk, not sure whether to run. Officer Ryan walked over to Rainbow. "Hey," she said.

No reaction. Rainbow sat with her head bowed and her hair falling into her lap.

"Can you get up?" Officer Ryan asked

Rainbow didn't answer.

Officer Ryan stepped closer, and pulled the long black baton from her belt.

"Don't hurt her," I said.

"I'm not going to," Officer Ryan answered. With the tip of

10 **to do a sweep:** eine Razzia machen. 13 **surgical gloves:** Latexhandschuhe (für Chirurgen). 16 **bowed:** gebeugt. 17 **lap:** Schoß. 20 **baton:** Schlagstock.

the baton she touched the side of Rainbow's leg. Rainbow jerked her head up, but her hair remained covering her face like a sheepdog.

"Can you get up?" Officer Ryan asked again.

Rainbow shook her head. You didn't see her face, just a mop of blond hair swaying back and forth.

"You're going in," Officer Ryan said. "Either get up by yourself or I'll have to get you up."

"I'll help her," I said. I didn't want Officer Ryan to touch Rainbow.

"I'll have to take you in, too," said Officer Ryan.

"I don't care."

Officer Ryan stepped back. "Be my guest."

I kneeled close enough to Rainbow to catch a strong whiff of her smell. It was sharp and bitter. "I'll go with you and make sure you're okay."

Rainbow raised her head. "My hero."

I slipped my hands under her arms and had to use all my strength to help her up. Shaking and unsteady, she got to her feet. I didn't let go because I was afraid she might fall. Her hair clung to her face like a mop, and her smell was like acid burning in my nose. Under her clothes her arms felt thin and bony, the flesh loose.

2 **to remain:** verharren, bleiben. 7 **you're going in:** du bist verhaftet. 11 **to take s.o. in:** jdn. einsperren. 14 **whiff:** Hauch. 19 **unsteady:** unsicher, schwankend. 22 **acid:** Säure.

I steered her toward the van. The rear windows had wire grating over them. Officer Ryan pulled open the doors. Under a plastic light in the ceiling I saw five others already inside sitting on two benches. They were all older. Some wore blond or red wigs and had faces painted like totem poles.

"You have to step up," I told Rainbow.

She didn't move.

"Come on," I said. "Pick up your foot."

She started to lift her foot, then lost her balance and began to fall. I tried to stop her, but then I started to fall, too. A pair of stronger hands caught my shoulders. It was Officer Ryan.

"I'll hold her," she said. "You get her in."

I climbed into the van and Officer Ryan guided Rainbow in. Me and Rainbow sat on the bench and Rainbow's head fell back and thumped against the wall. Her eyes never opened. Officer Ryan slammed the doors shut.

The van lurched. The back where we sat smelled sweet and sour. Perfume and urine. The others stared at Rainbow and me.

"Oh, look, it's kindergarten," sniggered a woman with a big, fluffy blond wig.

1 **rear window:** Heckscheibe. **wire grating:** Drahtgitter. 5 **totem pole:** Totempfahl. 15 **to climb:** (ein)steigen. 19 **to lurch:** schlingern.

"Shut up," another muttered. "Bet you was probably that young when you started."

"Not *that* young," huffed the fluffy blond. "And I never looked that fine."

"That's for *damned* sure," agreed a long-legged woman wearing a straight red wig. The others laughed.

The fluffy blond leaned toward Rainbow. "Let me see something."

I slid over, placing myself between her and Rainbow.

"Ooh, look, she got a protector," the fluffy blond said. "Whatsa matter, honey? You afraid I might do something to your friend?"

"Maybe."

"I ain't gonna hurt her." She extended a long, curved, fake red fingernail. It was shaped like a claw. "I just want to touch her. See if she's real."

I didn't budge. She wasn't going to touch Rainbow if I could stop her.

"Leave 'em alone," said the one with the long red wig.

The van stopped again. The doors opened and a woman with short straight black hair climbed on. She looked at Rainbow and me and sneered: "What's this, the school bus?"

10 **protector:** Beschützer(in). 11 **whatsa matter:** *what is the matter.* 14 **to extend:** ausstrecken. 15 **claw:** Klaue. 17 **to budge:** sich rühren. 22 **to sneer:** höhnisch lächeln.

At the police station Officer Ryan and a male police officer with a red moustache stood by the back door of the van and looked at each of us as we got out.

"You come with me." The male police officer pointed a finger at the long-legged woman with the long red wig.

"We going somewhere?" the woman asked with a suggestive wink.

"Yeah, over to the men's division."

Officer Ryan led the rest of us inside to a big cell. Rainbow was walking a little better by then. She pushed the hair out of her face. Her forehead was streaked with dirt and her sunken eyes had dark rings under them. The cell had a toilet sticking out of the wall in the corner. The toilet had no seat, but every time I looked someone was sitting on it. Rainbow slumped down in the corner and let her head dip. I sat next to her with my back against the cold concrete wall.

Officer Ryan and the policewoman with the black hair took people out of the cell one by one. When it was my turn Officer Ryan said, "Come on, there's someone I want you to talk to."

She took me down a narrow yellow hall and into a large room with lots of desks. Most of them were empty, but I

6 **suggestive:** auffordernd. 8 **men's division:** Abteilung für Männer. 15 **to slump:** fallen; sinken. **to dip:** heruntersinken. 16 **concrete:** Beton.

was led to one where a heavy man with gray hair sat at a computer. He wore a white shirt with thin blue stripes.

"This is Detective Charles," Officer Ryan said. "He's in charge of our youth program. I have to go back and process the others, but he'd like to talk to you."

Officer Ryan left. Det. Charles pointed to a scarred wooden chair beside his desk. "Have a seat."

I sat down.

"How old are you?" he asked.

"I forget."

He smirked. "What's your name?"

"I forget."

"How about your street name?"

"I forget."

"Bet you don't have any ID on you either."

Since it wasn't a question, I didn't have to answer. Detective Charles leaned forward and started to type on the computer. I looked at the framed pictures on his desk. Photos of him with a blond woman. Him with his arms around two tall thin boys with dark hair and his eyes. His sons. A happy family.

Det. Charles stopped typing on the computer and leaned back in his chair. He put his hands behind his head.

3 **to be in charge of:** leiten. 4 **to process:** abfertigen. 6 **Det.:** *Detective* (Kriminalbeamter). **scarred:** zerkratzt. 18 **framed:** gerahmt.

“So what are you? Fourteen? Fifteen?”

“I forget.”

“You know, I. Forget, right now you may still be young enough to get off the street. But you’re running out of time. Pretty soon there’ll be no going back.” He paused and waited to see if I’d answer. I didn’t.

“I ain’t talking about going back home,” he went on. “I’m talking about going back to society. Back to sleeping in a real bed instead of the sidewalk, and eating off a plate with a knife and fork instead of out of a Dumpster with your fingers. Back to getting new clothes in a store instead of the used rags they leave for you on the fence in front of the church. If I were you, I’d think about that, I. Forget. Because you’re getting pretty close to the point where you’re gonna forget a lot more than your name. You’re gonna forget how to be a human being. Then there’ll only be three places for you. Jail. The street. And in the ground.”

He paused again. When I didn’t say nothing, he said, “Or maybe it’s already too late. Maybe you’re too far gone. Maybe you already know all this and I’m just an old boring fart wasting both our time.”

I wasn’t even listening. I was thinking about Rainbow, all alone in that cell full of strangers.

4 **running out of time:** langsam keine Zeit mehr haben. 8 **society:** Gesellschaft. 17 **in the ground:** unter der Erde. 21 **old boring fart:** alter Langweiler.

"Hey, I. Forget," Det. Charles said. "Stay with me for one more second, okay?"

I looked at him. His face was shiny, almost like it was covered by a thin coat of oil. His nose was big and red and pitted, like a strawberry.

"You could have a life, understand?" he said. "You're still young enough to go back to school, learn a trade, whatever. You could have a place to live. A bed. A TV set. A refrigerator to put food in. Someday you could have a car. You could get off the street and go places. Let me ask you something, I. Forget. You ever seen the ocean?"

I nodded.

He scowled a little. "Where?"

"TV."

"Yeah, right. Only that's not the ocean, okay? That's just a picture. It ain't real. Like a picture of fire don't feel hot. You gotta see it in person. You gotta feel it and smell it. I don't care what you've seen on TV or in the movies. You ain't seen the ocean unless you've stood with your feet in the sand and the waves washing up to your knees. You know, they say life came from the ocean, and I believe it. You get out there and you feel that water run over you and you smell that salt spray in the air, and it's like you're right back at the

7 **to learn a trade:** einen Beruf erlernen. 13 **to scowl:** ein finsteres Gesicht machen. 23 **salt spray:** salzige Gischt.

beginning of time. You look at those waves and the sky and the clouds and sun and all that water. Endless amounts of water. And you feel like you could wash in it. Wash away everything bad. Every crappy unfair thing that ever happened to you, gone. Then you could start all over again. A whole new beginning just like the day you were born. You could do it, I. Forget. Start over. You think that miserable, dirty, hungry street world out there is the only life there is for you, but it ain't. There's other lives. Plenty of 'em. You can get out of here and go someplace else. Anywhere, you want, I. Forget."

I was listening. I was there, at the edge of that ocean I never been to. My bare feet sinking in sand they never stood in, feeling the ocean water I never felt.

"I want you to do me a favor, okay, I. Forget?" Det. Charles said. "I want you to think about it, and if you decide you want to go see the ocean, you come back here and tell me, okay?"

He leaned forward in his chair and reached into his jacket pocket, pulled out an old brown leather wallet and took out a white business card. He handed it to me.

"Don't forget, I. Forget," he said. "This ain't the only life.

4 **crappy:** beschissen. 7 **miserable:** elend; fürchterlich. 15 **do me a favor:** tu mir einen Gefallen. 20 **wallet:** Brieftasche. 21 **business card:** Visitenkarte.

There's plenty others. And, believe me, all of them are a damn lot better."

He took me back to the cell. The others weren't happy to see me.

"Look what your friend did," the fluffy blond said.

Rainbow was lying on the floor, her face at the edge of a small pool of yellowish, smelly puke. I went over and helped her sit up. She opened her eyes for a moment, then closed them again. I used the sleeve of my sweatshirt to wipe the mess off Rainbow's face and off the collar of her leather jacket. The smell was harsh and strong and made me feel like barfing, too.

The woman with the short black hair came over. "It's a good thing she was lying on her side. That happens when she's on her back and she'll breathe it into her lungs and choke to death."

"What you gonna do about that?" The fluffy blond pointed at the yellow puddle on the floor.

I pulled off my sweatshirt and laid it over the puddle. Then I sat with my back against the wall and Rainbow's head in my lap, waiting for whatever happened next.

7 **puke:** Kotze. 12 **barfing:** Kotzen. 16 **choke to death:** ersticken.

SEVENTEEN

I stroked Rainbow's hair. It was knotted and filthy. I picked out some of the bigger pieces of dirt and tried to undo some of the smaller tangles without pulling on her hair hard enough to hurt her. Rainbow's lips were cracked and scabbed. Drool dripped out of the corner of her mouth, and I wiped it away with the bottom of my T-shirt.

Around the cell the women talked about what they did and how they were treated.

"When I get out of here I'm leaving town. This is the last night I'm spending in jail."

"That man takes every penny I make."

"All I gotta do is kick the junk and I'm outta this life."

"Anyone know what time it is?" the small woman with the short black hair asked.

"Why, you got a date?" smirked the fluffy blond. No one knew the time. I never thought about it nomore. Not in

8 **to stroke:** streicheln. 10 **tangle:** Gewirr. 11 **cracked:** gerissen. 12 **scabbed:** schorfig. **drool:** Speichel. 19 **to kick the junk:** aufhören Heroin zu nehmen. **I'm outta this life:** ich lasse dieses ganze Leben (das ich jetzt führe) hinter mir. 22 **you got a date?:** Hast du eine Verabredung?

hours or minutes or seconds, at least. Instead there was sleeping time and waking time. There was begging for money time and the time when you ate or scored drugs or drank. There was day time and night time. Time when you were scared and time when your stomach hurt. There was feeling cold or sick time and time when you felt okay.

"Anyone seen that show, *Sex in the City*?" someone asked. The women hooted and yelled and laughed. Oh, yeah, they'd all seen it. Plenty of times. Every night. I knew they meant something different than what the woman had asked. I'd heard of that show but I'd never seen it. I didn't even know what was on TV anymore. Oh, the *Simpsons* probably. And MTV.

Sometimes when Maggot talked about all the poor people and the revolution I would wonder about the rest of the world. The world away from the street. What happened yesterday? Was there a war somewhere? Did terrorists blow up another building? Did they discover life on another planet? I never wondered for long because then I got hungry and had to look for something to eat. Or I got cold or I needed money. I guess that's why homeless kids don't go to school. They're too busy just trying to stay alive.

The cell door opened and Officer Ryan and the lady cop

3 **to score drugs:** Drogen beschaffen. 8 **to hoot:** johlen. 15 **to wonder:** sich fragen. 17 **to blow up:** in die Luft sprengen. 22 **busy:** beschäftigt.

with the black hair came in, their black belts' flashlights and nightsticks thumping against their thighs. They started toward us. I stopped breathing. They were coming for Rainbow.

I slid my arms around Rainbow's body. The policewomen stood over us with their hands on their hips.

"Can she get up?" Officer Ryan asked.

"I don't think so."

"Tell her you got some rock," said the blond bitch. "She get right up fast."

"Back off," Officer Ryan warned. She kneeled closer and reached toward Rainbow's face. "Let's see if we can wake her."

"Don't touch her," I said.

"We have to see if she's okay."

"She's okay," I said.

"She could be OD'ing right now."

I shook my head. "I would know."

"You have to let us take her," Officer Ryan said. "See those plastic bands on her wrists? That means she left a hospital without permission. We have to follow up on that."

I tightened my arms around her. Rainbow was all I had in the world. If they took her away I might never see her again.

2 **nightstick:** Schlagstock. **to thump:** klopfen, schlagen. **thigh:** Schenkel. 9 **rock:** Crack. **bitch:** Miststück. 11 **Back off:** Halt dich zurück. 17 **OD'ing** (overdosing): eine Überdosis nehmen oder genommen haben. 21 **permission:** Erlaubnis. **we have to follow up on that:** dem müssen wir nachgehen.

The policewoman with the black hair glared down at me impatiently. "I'm only gonna tell you this once. Let her go … now."

I held on, feeling Rainbow's chest expand and contract as she breathed. I knew she wasn't OD'ing and didn't need to go nowhere.

"If that's the way you want it." The black-haired policewoman started to reach down, as if she was going to tear Rainbow out of my arms.

Officer Ryan said, "Don't."

"For God's sake, Jane," the black-haired policewoman sputtered.

Still kneeling in front of us, Officer Ryan spoke softly. "We have to take your friend. She may need medical attention. You have to let her go. Trust me. We want to help her. She'll be okay."

She sounded like she meant it. Only, that's what grown-ups did so well. They knew how to sound like they meant everything they said. But then they changed their minds. Or, more likely, they never really meant it in the first place. They were just lying to get you to do what they wanted. So you learned not to believe them. You learned to take what they gave when they were nice. But to always be ready for them

1 **to glare down:** zornig herunterstarren. 2 **impatiently** (adv.): ungeduldig. 4 **to expand:** sich ausdehnen. **to contract:** sich zusammenziehen. 13 **to kneel:** knien. 23 **always be ready for them to turn on you:** sei immer darauf vorbereitet, dass sie sich gegen dich wenden.

to turn on you. Because ninety-nine percent of the time that's exactly what they did.

The black-haired policewoman muscled in. "Look," she growled at me, "either you let go of her or I get rough. Either way she's going with us. Just depends on how bad you want to get hurt in the process."

I hardly cared about being hurt. Been hurt plenty. But letting go of Rainbow would really hurt. I held on to her. "She's okay."

"I don't have time for this," the black-haired policewoman complained. "Either you let go of her right now or you're gonna be sorry."

"Come on, hon, be a good kid and let her go." Officer Ryan reached toward Rainbow. "I promise we'll take good care of her. Don't you want your friend to be okay?" She put her hands on mine. She was still wearing those latex gloves.

"I'll never see her again," I whimpered.

Officer Ryan's eyebrows dipped with sympathy. "You really care about her, don't you?"

I nodded. "She's one of us. Belongs to the Asphalt Tribe."

"Asphalt Tribe. That's the name of your gang – the boy dealing with baking powder, the guy with the dog and you girls.

4 **to get rough:** ungemütlich werden. 5 **to depend:** abhängen. 11 **to complain:** sich beklagen. 13 **hon** (honey): Schätzchen. 17 **to whimper:** wimmern.

"Yeah, exactly."

"For God's sake, Jane," the black-haired policewoman grumbled like this was a total waste of her time.

Officer Ryan looked into my eyes. It was a different look than before. I can't explain it, but I could feel it. "Listen, I'm sorry I have to do this, but it's my job. I promise I'll tell you where she is so you'll be able to find each other. Okay?"

"You swear?" I said.

"Cross my heart." Officer Ryan closed her hands around mine and slowly, gently lifted them off Rainbow. She carefully pulled Rainbow to her feet. One of Rainbow's sleeves slid back.

"Oh!" Officer Ryan caught her breath when she saw all the cuts and scabs on Rainbow's arms.

"Yeah, they cut themselves," the black-haired policewoman said. "Always freaks me out, too. But a lot of them do it. The girls especially."

Holding Rainbow by the arms, Officer Ryan and the black-haired policewoman led her away. Rainbow half walked and half allowed herself be pulled along, sometimes taking a step, sometimes letting the toes of her shoes scrape on the floor.

The fluffy blond came over. She put her hands on her hips

8 **to swear:** schwören. 9 **Cross my heart:** Ehrenwort. 10 **gently** (adv.): vorsichtig. 13 **to catch one's breath:** tief Luft holen.

and turned so that she was looking over her shoulder at me. "Child, do you know how bad you just got played? They ran the oldest cop trick in the book. Good cop, bad cop. One acts all rough and mean to make you hate her and the other acts all sweet and nice to make you like her. Next thing you know, you want to do the nice one a favor just to show the mean one whose side you're on. You really believe that crap about them telling you where your friend is going? Honey, they don't give a hoot about you or your friend. They just can't let junkies die in jail. That's real bad publicity, understand? That girl cop ain't gonna tell you nothin'. She just doin' her job. Next time they play that game, I bet the black-haired one'll be all sweetness and the blond will be the mean, nasty one. They do it to get what they want, honey."

The tears came faster and I felt my lower lip start to quiver. I didn't want to believe what she was saying, but I knew it was most likely true.

The small woman with the short black hair came over. "What's the point of telling her that?" she demanded of the fluffy blond. "You knew they were gonna take that little junky girl no matter what. So why you tryin' to make this girl feel bad now? What good is that?"

2 **to get played:** an der Nase herumgeführt werden. 4 **one acts all rough and mean:** eine(r) zieht die harte Nummer ab. 9 **they don't give a hoot about you:** du bist denen völlig Schnuppe. 10 **publicity:** Werbung. 14 **nasty:** böse; widerlich. 16 **to quiver:** zittern. 22 **no matter what:** egal was passiert.

"I'm just tellin' her how it works."

"Oh, sure. Like you know that police lady ain't gonna come back and tell her where they send the little junky girl."

"You think she will?"

"I seen stranger things," replied the smaller woman. "And even if she don't, why you gotta be the one to spread the bad news?"

By then it didn't matter what either of them said. What mattered was that Rainbow was gone and I felt empty and alone in a cold cell filled with strangers, in a cold city filled with strangers, in a cold world.

I put my hand in my pocket and felt the card Det. Charles gave me. I took it out and tore it into little pieces.

6 **to spread:** verbreiten. 13 **to tear, tore, torn:** zerreißen.

EIGHTEEN

I fell asleep. When I woke up most of the women who'd been in the cell the night before were gone, and a whole new bunch was there. The fluffy blond and the small woman with the black hair were gone. Rainbow was gone. I had to go to the bathroom really bad, but I didn't want to use the toilet in front of all those women so I lay on the floor in the corner and waited. I felt dried salt trails in the corners of my eyes and wondered if I'd cried in my sleep.

After a while a policewoman came in. She had red hair and was so skinny that even her heavy gun belt didn't make her look fat. She pointed at me. "You. Come on, let's go."

I got up slowly and followed her out of the cell and into the hall.

"What's your name?" she asked.

"Maybe."

"Huh?"

"They call me Maybe. It's my name."

12 **really bad:** ganz dringend. 14 **trail:** Spur. 17 **skinny:** dürr. 18 **to point at:** zeigen auf.

"What about your real name?"

"It is my real name."

"Okay, Maybe, you know where we're going?"

I yawned. "To the bathroom, I hope."

She stopped. "What about the cell? Oh, you didn't want to go in front of all those ladies, right?"

"So could I go now?"

"Sure, Maybe, but I'm gonna have to come in there with you. Gotta make sure there's no funny stuff."

We went into the bathroom and I let myself into a stall. "Is Officer Ryan here?" I asked.

"Her shift ended," the policewoman answered. "She's gone."

I felt a stab in my heart. It figured that she left without telling me where they took Rainbow. The blond bitch was right. I got played big time. Back out into the hall the red-haired policewoman said, "Back to my original question. You know where you're going?"

I shook my head.

"You want to know?"

I shrugged. What difference did it make? At the end of the hall she pushed open a door and I followed her into a large room with a lot of chairs and benches. A woman with long

9 **make sure there is no funny stuff:** auf Nummer sicher gehen. 10 **stall:** Kabine. 12 **shift:** Schicht. 14 **stab:** Stich. **It figured:** es war einleuchtend. 16 **I got played big time:** ich war komplett verarscht worden. 23 **bench:** (Sitz-)Bank.

brown hair was sitting in one of the benches. She was wearing a bright red wool cap and puffy light blue parka. When she saw us she got up.

"Hi, my name's Laura and I'm from the Youth Housing Project. What's your name?"

I recognized her voice. She was the female flashlight. I told her my name was Maybe.

"You look familiar," Laura said. "Have I ever seen you before?"

"Maybe."

She smiled. "I bet that's your answer to a lot of questions."

I could have answered maybe, but I didn't. We went through a door to the outside. Since I just woke up I thought it was morning, but from the way the sun was behind the buildings, I could see that it was afternoon. And cold. I left the sweatshirt in the cell. All I had on was the white T-shirt. I could not remember where I left the brown sweater Anthony gave me. Goose bumps rose on my arms, and I began to shiver.

"That's all you've got?" Laura asked as we stopped next to a dented blue van that said Youth Housing Project on the side. She opened the back door and took out a navy blue blanket. "Put it around your shoulders. It'll keep you warm until we get to the project."

2 **puffy:** bauschig. 6 **to recognize:** erkennnen. 8 **familiar:** bekannt. 21 **dented:** verbeult.

The blanket was thinner than I expected, but I was glad to have it. We got into the van. It smelled like coffee. Some empty white Styrofoam cups lay on the floor between the front seats.

Laura started to drive. "Do you know anything about the Youth Housing Project?"

"You got a lot of rules."

Laura frowned. "What makes you think that?"

"You told me."

The lines between her eyes deepened. "That rainy night a few weeks ago you were in that building off Avenue C?"

"Yeah."

"So which of our rules would be so hard for you to live with?" Laura said.

"I don't know. All of them."

"I don't think we have that many. Just what the state demands in order to get our funding. Don't you think it's worth agreeing to a few rules so that you can have a clean bed and clothes and a roof over your head?"

"Maybe."

"Why not give it a try, okay? We'll give you a bath and a meal and a comfortable bed. What could be so bad about that?"

"I don't know."

3 **Styrofoam:** Styropor. 17 **funding:** Mittel, Gelder. 18 **to agree to s.th.:** mit etw. einverstanden sein. 21 **to give it a try:** es einmal versuchen.

NINETEEN

The Youth Housing Project was in a four-story brick building on Avenue B. I got to wash and put on clean clothes. The other kids said hello, and then went back to watching TV. They didn't stare at my skin the way some strangers did. Maybe they were used to kids who looked different. At dinner I sat at a round table with five other kids and ate spaghetti with meatballs. The girl next to me had dyed black hair with blond roots and purple highlights, studs and bars through her eyebrows, nose, lips, ears, and tongue, and tattoos on the fingers of both hands. The letters on her right hand spelled LOVE and those on her left spelled HATE. Her name was Spyder and when she asked where I was from I said, "Nowhere and everywhere."

She nodded and said, "Right," like that made perfect sense. After dinner we watched more TV and then they told us it was time to go to bed. I didn't care because I was tired.

8 **brick:** Ziegelstein. 14 **meatball:** Fleischklößchen. 15 **root:** Wurzel. **studs and bars:** Piercings. 18 **to spell:** buchstabieren.

We went upstairs to a room with three bunk beds and open cubbies for clothes. My bed was in the bunk under Spyder's. The other girls changed into pajamas or baggy T-shirts, but I had nothing to sleep in.

"Here." Spyder tossed me a black Megadeath T-shirt.

"Thanks." I undressed and pulled it on and got into the bunk bed. It was the first time I been in a real bed since I'd left home. As I pulled the blanket up to my chin, and my head sank into the soft pillow, I felt myself relax. It wasn't only that the bed was comfortable. It was the feeling that I was safe for the night – a feeling I'd forgotten. I listened to Spyder and the other girls talk for a little while, but I fell asleep pretty fast because the next thing I knew, the room was filled with sunlight and Laura was in the doorway saying it was time to get up.

Still tired and wanting to go back to sleep I pulled the pillow over my head. A hand touched my shoulder.

"You have to get up now," Laura said.

"I'm tired."

"It's time for breakfast. Aren't you hungry?"

My stomach felt empty, so even though I wanted to sleep, I got up and went downstairs. I sat next to Spyder at the round table and had cold cereal and juice for breakfast.

1 **bunk beds:** Etagenbett. **cubby:** Fach. 14 **to be in the doorway:** in der Tür stehen. 23 **cereal:** Müsli, Frühstücksflocken. **juice:** Saft.

Then it was time to sit in a circle and talk about our lives. Laura said I didn't have to, but she urged me to join in. All I could think about was that soft pillow and those smooth warm sheets.

"I want to go back upstairs," I said.

"That's not allowed," Laura said. "If you have to sleep, you can sleep down here."

A bunch of kids gathered in a circle to talk. Most looked a few years older than me. Like Spyder, they had tattoos and piercings and dyed hair. They sort of looked like street kids, only cleaned up. All the chairs and spots on the couch were taken so I lay down on the floor and tried to close my eyes. It wasn't easy to sleep with everyone talking, and it wasn't nearly as comfortable as the bunk bed upstairs. Then they turned on the TV and watched until lunch. Only I wasn't hungry.

"You still have to sit with everyone at the table," Laura said.

After lunch they wanted us to do an art project with feathers and string and pieces of wire. Laura said I didn't have to, so I just sat there. Spyder smiled, but the other kids mostly ignored me. By then I was hungry again and wanted something to eat, but Laura said I had to wait until dinner.

I waited until she left the room. Then I took a black ski jacket from the closet and left.

2 **to urge s.o.:** jdn. eindringlich bitten; jdn. drängen. **to join in:** mitmachen. 8 **to gather:** sich versammeln. 19 **string:** Schnur, Kordel. **wire:** Draht. 24 **closet:** Wandschrank.

It was getting dark when I got back to the bridge. OG had hung the blue tarp again and Pest, Maggot, and Jewel were inside. Jewel was rocking back and forth and staring up at nothing. Someone else was in the orange sleeping bag. My heart jumped for a second at the thought that it might be Rainbow. I looked closer. It was Tears.

"Hey," I said.

"Hey." Her answer was as hollow as her eyes.

"Where you been?" I asked.

"Nowhere."

"That night at *The Cradle*," I said, "I came back to look for you and you were gone."

Tears turned her face away and pulled the sleeping bag over her head.

"Where've you been?" Maggot asked me.

"Rainbow got picked up by the cops and I went with her," I said. "Anyone seen her?"

No one answered.

"Then they sent me to the Youth Housing Project," I said.

Jewel smiled. "Did you enjoy the accommodations, my dear?"

"I liked sleeping in a real bed again."

"Then why'd you leave?" Maggot asked.

8 **hollow:** hohl, leer. 16 **to get picked up:** verhaftet werden. 20 **accommodations:** Unterkunft.

"Too many rules about when you could sleep and eat."

"So it's not just about their state funding, right?" Maggot asked.

I shook my head. "I don't see why the state would care when I eat or sleep."

"It's all about decorum, darling," Jewel said as he rocked. "Nice appearance, good manners, etcetera, etcetera."

"It's all about fear of anyone different," said OG.

"Right and it's all about brainwashing you to fit in," Maggot said.

It got dark, and the temperature must have dropped twenty degrees. Like animals, we burrowed into our nests of blankets and newspapers and plastic bags, and curled up close to each other to stay warm.

But I hardly got to sleep. Maggot coughed all the time. Jewel sneezed and mumbled to himself. Tears cried. OG was sick. The cars roared above. In the moonlight jagged hunks of snow-covered ice floated down the river like icebergs. I watched the sun come up. The tops of the buildings started to glow. Bursts of red morning sunlight reflected off the windows. The murky green-brown river turned a lighter shade.

6 **decorum:** Anstand, äußerer Anschein. 9 **to brainwash:** eine Gehirnwäsche verabreichen. **to fit in:** sich anpassen, dazupassen. 12 **to burrow:** graben, buddeln. 13 **to curl up:** sich zusammenrollen. **close to:** nahe bei. 22 **shade:** (Farb-)ton.

Maggot sat up. "I have to get some cough medicine. Anyone have any money?"

"Plenty, darling," Jewel said, still rocking back and forth and staring off. "As much as you need. The family comes from royalty, you know. It's all in offshore accounts."

Maggot rolled his eyes. "Anyone *else* have any money?"

"Just the squeegee," OG said and coughed so hard he had to put his hands on the ground to brace himself.

We took turns trying to get drivers to pay us for cleaning their windshields. When you stood out in the traffic the icy wind blew right through your clothes. The streets were slippery and you had to be careful not to fall and get run over. When it was my turn I waited on the corner until the light turned red, then picked up the bucket and walked between the cars. No one wanted his windshield washed. Here and there a driver gave me a quarter anyway. One man in an expensive-looking car rolled down his window and thrust a dollar out.

"Just don't wash my windshield, okay?" he begged.

The light turned green and I hurried back to the corner, trying to avoid the cars. Loose sheets of newspaper blew past and the traffic lights above swung like fruit on a tree. It was so cold my nose and ears stung. The drivers passed and

5 **royalty:** Königshaus. **offshore account:** Überseekonto. 8 **to brace oneself:** sich abstützen. 9 **to take turns:** sich abwechseln. 23 **to sting, stung, stung:** stechen.

didn't even look. I was nothing. A creature without a name who nobody cared about. One of the unlucky ones who got left behind when the big bus of happy families pulled out of the bus station. There wasn't even room for me on the big bus of unhappy families. There wasn't room, period.

The dirty water in the bucket froze into a brownish block. I went back to the bridge and crawled into my nest and lay there quivering. After a while OG came back with a metal garbage can he stole from a nearby building. He tried to start a fire in it, but the newspaper burned up so fast it was gone before we could get warm.

"We have to find some wood," Maggot said through chattering teeth. "I think I saw some at a construction site up by the park." He and OG went to look for wood. Tears and I stayed behind with Pest, who lay inside my nest with me. Over the river the sea gulls slowly flapped their wings higher and higher, then glided in circles back down. I heard sobs coming from the nest Tears had made for herself.

"Hey, Tears," I called. "What's wrong?"

"I wet the sleeping bag. It's cold."

"Come over here with Pest and me. You'll feel warmer."

"But I'm wet."

"Who cares?"

5 **period:** Schluss. 13 **construction site:** Baustelle. 16 **to flap:** schlagen. **wing:** Flügel. 17 **to glide:** gleiten.

She crawled out of the sleeping bag and into my nest of blankets and papers. We lay on our sides with Pest between us. I wondered about Rainbow and felt an ache when I thought about Officer Ryan and that other policewoman taking her away.

Tears shook so hard she made the newspapers around us rattle. Her teeth chattered. She started to cry again. "I want to go home."

"You can go over to the Youth Housing Project," I said. "That lady Laura could help you find your mom."

"I can't. Not as long as he's there."

"Your stepfather? Maybe he's gone. When was the last time you talked to your mom?"

"I don't know. A long time ago."

"Maybe you should call her."

"How? I don't got any money."

"Collect."

"Last time I did that she got mad and told me not to no more. I don't want to make her mad because then she won't want me back."

I knew if we went to the Youth Housing Project Laura might let Tears use the phone. But I also knew that Laura might give Tears a hard time about going back to the street. It's

3 **ache:** Schmerz. 7 **to rattle:** klappern. 17 **Collect:** R-Gespräch (der Angerufene zahlt). 18 **to get mad:** wütend werden. 23 **to give s.o. a hard time:** jdm. das Leben schwer machen.

one thing when you're 15 or 16. You're halfway to being a grown up and if you want to be on the street they know they can't stop you. It's different when you're 12. Then they think you're still a kid.

I had another idea. "There's a place where you might be able to make the call," I said. "We could go see."

"Let me get a little warmer first, okay?"

I opened the black ski jacket and tried to pull some of it around Tears. That seemed to help. When her teeth stopped chattering we got up and headed for the library.

When we got there, Bobby was outside using a plastic cup from which he scooped white crystals onto the library steps to melt the ice. I stopped on the sidewalk.

"Aren't we going in?" Tears asked, hugging herself to stay warm.

"We better wait," I said.

Tears looked at Bobby. "It's him, right?"

I nodded and felt sad. Tears was turning into a street kid. She was starting to get that street sense of who was dangerous and who wasn't. In my head I could hear the words of that detective: "*You're running out of time. Pretty soon there'll be no going back.*" How soon was pretty soon? Were we already too late? We stood in the cold and waited.

10 **to head for:** gehen, fahren in Richtung. 13 **to melt:** schmelzen. 18 **to turn into:** sich (ver)wandeln. 19 **sense of:** Gefühl für, Sinn für.

Bobby didn't look in our direction. After a while he went back into the library.

"Can we go in now?" Tears asked.

"I have to see something first." I looked in the big windows. People were sitting at the computers. Anthony was standing behind a white-haired man who was frowning at a computer screen. Anthony said something to him. Still frowning, the man typed on the keyboard. Something good must have happened because the man's face brightened. Anthony smiled and started to move down the table. That's when he looked up and saw me outside.

He waved like he wanted me to come in. I shook my head. He raised a finger as if to say, "Wait one second." I went back to Tears, who was shivering.

"I'm cold," she said. "Can't we go in?"

"In a second, I hope."

A minute later Anthony came out wearing a green coat. It was unbuttoned and he held it closed with both hands. "What's up?"

"My friend needs to make an important telephone call," I said.

Anthony didn't answer right away. He must have been thinking about whether he could let Tears use the phone. "Okay, come in."

1 **direction:** Richtung. 8 **to type:** tippen. **keyboard:** Tastatur. 9 **to brighten:** sich aufhellen.

"What about Bobby?" I asked.

"Don't worry about him."

Anthony held the door. It was warm inside. Somewhere a radiator hissed. I looked for Bobby, but he wasn't around. Anthony led us past the counter where the frowning people with the ID tags stood, to a door in the back. Inside was a hall lined with more doors. Anthony pushed one open, and we went into a small office with lots of books on shelves and a desk with a computer and stacks of papers. A glass bowl was filled with jelly beans of every color imaginable.

"Hold out your hands," Anthony said. He picked up the bowl and poured some jelly beans into our palms. While Tears and I ate them, Anthony pressed some numbers on the phone and waited. On his desk were pictures of two girls. One about Tears's age and one maybe eight years old. In some of the pictures they were with a man and a woman who had red hair and freckles like Anthony, but not the blotches Anthony and I both had.

Anthony handed the phone to Tears. "I've got you an outside line. You can dial your number."

Tears dialed and held the phone to her ear. "Mom? It's Nikki. Hey, yeah, I'm okay. In New York. Yeah, it's really cold. No, I'm warm enough. Oh, here and there. No, noth-

4 **to hiss:** zischen. 9 **stacks of papers:** Papierstapel. 10 **jelly beans:** Geleebonbon, Weingummibonbon. 19 **outside line:** Amtsleitung. 20 **to dial:** wählen.

ing like that. Yeah, I want to come home. Is he still living there? I told you why. No, Mom. He did. I don't care what he says. No, I didn't imagine it. Then he's a liar. No, I won't come home as long as he's there. I don't think so. Okay, have it your way. Bye."

She hung up and tears began to roll down her cheeks. She looked at me and shook her head. Then she turned to Anthony. "Thanks for letting me use the phone."

"You're welcome." Anthony pulled a moist wipe out of a plastic container and wiped off the receiver before putting it back on the cradle. "I guess it wasn't much help."

Tears wiped her eyes with her hands, leaving dirty smears.

"We really appreciate you letting her try," I said.

"Anytime," Anthony said. "But now I have to get back to the computer tables."

I looked nervously at the door and wondered if Bobby was on the other side. Anthony saw me. "Let me take you out." He held the door and led us back down the hall. "You don't have to leave, you know. You're welcome to stay here all day. There are couches to sit on and books and magazines to read." He opened the door to the main library, and we went back out.

"What the hell?" Bobby came out from between a row of

3 **liar:** Lügner. 5 **have it your way:** Wie du willst. 9 **moist:** feucht. **wipe:** Tuch. 10 **receiver:** Hörer. 11 **cradle:** Gabel. 13 **to appreciate:** zu schätzen wissen.

bookshelves. I jumped back and banged into Tears, who let out a cry. Anthony quickly stepped between Bobby and us.

"Is there a problem?" he asked Bobby.

"What do you want them in here for?" Bobby asked.

"This library is open to the public, Bob."

"But they're not ..." Bobby didn't finish the sentence.

"Not what?" Anthony asked.

"You know," Bobby sputtered. "Don't pretend, Anthony. They're just gonna make a mess."

Anthony turned to Tears and me. "Are you going to make a mess?"

We shook our heads.

"Aw, for Pete's sake." Bobby grumbled. "Of course they're going to say that."

"I believe them," Anthony said.

Bobby narrowed his eyes at Tears and me. "I'll be watching you." He turned and went off.

Anthony led us toward the front. "You can sit near the computer tables if you like. That way you can be close to me."

Tears and me shared a look. We didn't want to go back out into the cold, but Bobby scared us.

"We have to go somewhere," I said.

The corners of Anthony's mouth turned down, but he

5 **open to the public:** der Öffentlichkeit zugänglich. 8 **to sputter:** zischen; sich ereifern. 10 **to make a mess:** Unordnung machen; eine Schweinerei anrichten. 13 **for Pete's sake:** um Himmels willen. 21 **to scare s.o.:** jdm. Angst einjagen.

walked with us to the front doors. “Wait,” he said, like he remembered something. “I’ll be right back.” He turned and went back toward his office.

“Where’s he going?” Tears asked.

“I don’t know,” I said. “But let’s wait outside.”

We went out into the cold. People were wearing heavy coats and gloves and hats and scarves wrapped tightly around their necks. Tears and I hugged ourselves and waited. After a little while Anthony came back through the main doors carrying a box of donuts. “We had a little party at lunch today and these were left over.”

“Thanks,” I said.

A gust of wind made our clothes flap. Tears and I turned our backs to it.

“You really can stay, you know,” Anthony said. “I promise Bobby will leave you alone.”

“Thanks,” I said. “Maybe another time.”

Anthony smiled sadly. “Okay, just don’t be strangers. Either of you.”

Tears and me headed down the sidewalk, eating the donuts. “You think he’s nice to you because he has the same skin thing?” Tears asked.

“No,” I said. “I think he’s just nice.”

8 **to hug oneself:** die Arme verschränken, sich die Arme reiben. 13 **gust of wind:** Windbö.

TWENTY

Smoke was blowing from under the bridge where the tarp was. Tears and me saw it from almost two blocks away. For a second I got scared, then I remembered that OG and Maggot went to find wood for a fire. Blackened pieces of wood sticking out of the garbage can and orange flames shooting up. OG and Maggot were standing close to the fire, warming their hands and coughing.

"Look, fire! Warmth!" Maggot cried when he saw us. Pest barked. Tears and I joined them around the garbage can and held our hands out. The swirling wind pushed the smoke this way and that, and we kept moving to stay out of the way.

"Where's the pig? We need a pig to roast!" Maggot cried. "We'll kill the pig." He pulled a burning stick out of the fire and held it like a spear. He started to chant, "Kill the beast! Cut his throat! Spill his blood!"

17 **swirling:** wirbelnd. 18 **this way and that:** hin und her. 22 **spear:** Speer. **to chant:** im Sprechchor singen. 23 **to spill blood:** Blut vergießen.

"What pig?" I asked.

Maggot threw the stick back into the garbage can. A flurry of orange sparks flew out. "*Lord of the Flies*."

"What's that?" Tears asked.

Maggot turned to OG. "You've heard of it, right?"

OG frowned. "Was it a TV show or something?"

"You total freaks." Maggot sounded disgusted. "It's one of the most famous books ever written. About this bunch of kids who crash on an island and how some of them turn into savages."

"Like us," I said.

"Kind of," Maggot said.

"They killed each other. It was so primitive," said Jewel. He was sitting against the wall with his knees pulled up tight to his chest, rocking back and forth. "But you know what they say: Boys will be boys."

"You read it, Jewel?" Maggot asked.

"Oh, yes, darling. In school," Jewel said. "Everybody had to read it. It was required. I went to Exeter, you know. All the best children went there."

"All the best children," OG repeated.

"Everyone had trust funds," Jewel said. "And the places we'd go on vacation. The Vineyard. St. Barts. Capri. 2Moro

2 **flurry:** Gestöber; Stoß. 3 **sparks:** Funken. 10 **savages:** Wilde. 16 **Boys will be boys:** Jungen sind nun mal so. 19 **required:** vorgeschrieben. **Exeter:** teure Privatschule. 22 **trust fund:** Treuhandvermögen. 23 **The Vineyard, St. Barts, Capri:** exklusive Ferienorte in den USA und Italien.

and I were planning a getaway on my father's Gulfstream. But 2Moro's dead. So sad. Why didn't anyone tell me?"

For a long moment no one spoke. Then Maggot said, "Guess we didn't think it would make a difference."

"It makes a difference to me, my dear," Jewel said with a sniff. "She was my twin sister. Don't you think we should tell our parents? They'll be devastated. Just devastated. But life goes on, and they still have me and Piper and Christoff. Did I tell you we're spending Christmas in St. Moritz this year? Then off to Mykonos for New Year's Eve."

"That's great, Jewel," Maggot said. "Only New Year's Eve was three weeks ago."

1 **getaway:** Flucht. **Gulfstream:** Jachttyp. 6 **sniff:** Schniefen. 7 **devastated:** am Boden zerstört. 10 **Mykonos:** griechische Insel in der Ägäis.

TWENTY-ONE

Mary Ellen Golding, aka Rainbow, *born in North Miami Beach, Florida. Parents divorced when she was eight. Father remarried. Mother chronic alcoholic and drug addict. Age 11, removed from home after report that mother had exchanged her for drugs. Placed in foster care while mother in rehab. Age 12, returned to mother. Three months later mother relapsed, again exchanged Mary Ellen for drugs. Again placed in foster care. Age 14, diagnosed with OCD and depression. Medicated. Frequent behavioral problems in school. Chronic absences and truancy. Arrests for loitering and possession of narcotics. Age 15, served six months in juvenile correction facility. Age 16, reported missing. Last known address, New York City. Dead at the age of 16. Cause of death: Suicide.*

13 **rehab:** Rehabilitationszentrum. 14 **to relapse:** einen Rückfall haben. 16 **OCD:** Zwangsneurose. 18 **truancy:** Schulschwänzen. **loitering:** unberechtigter Aufenthalt.

You couldn't escape the cold. We shivered all the time. The brown ice in the squeegee bucket was rock hard. The river was jammed solid with snow-covered chunks. Someone said they were serving soup and sandwiches at the church. I went over there, but the line outside was too long and it was too cold to stand still.

I walked and walked, then stopped outside a store near Bleeker Street that sold television sets. They had one that almost filled a whole window. It was only a few inches thick and the colors on its screen were so bright they didn't seem real.

In the window's reflection I saw a police car pull up to the curb. Officer Ryan put on her hat and got out.

"I've been looking for you." Her breath came out like a cloud. "Aren't you cold?"

"Maybe," I said.

"Hungry?"

"Maybe."

She pointed to a diner a few doors down from the TV store. "Come on, let's get you something to eat."

I didn't move.

"You said you'd tell me where Rainbow went," I said.

Officer Ryan nodded. "I know. I'll tell you inside."

3 **chunk:** Brocken. 12 **to pull up to the curb:** am Straßenrand anhalten. 19 **diner**: Esslokal.

A gust of wind made the street signs twist. The sky was dark gray and the air felt like it was going to snow.

Officer Ryan gazed at me for a moment, like she was realizing that more than warmth and food, what I really needed was the truth.

"Why do you want to buy me something to eat?" I asked.

"Because you look hungry."

"And that's it? I get something to eat and then I can go? No tricks?"

"No tricks."

The diner's windows were fogged with frost. We went in and sat in a booth. Some of the people sitting near the windows still wore their coats and hats, so it probably wasn't that warm, but to me it felt hot compared to the outside. A waitress wearing a fuzzy light blue sweater came over and gave us menus. She sniffed the air around me and wrinkled her nose. Then her eyes went soft and sad.

"Just coffee," Officer Ryan said without opening the menu. To me she said, "Order whatever you want."

On the cover of the menu was a picture of a stack of pancakes covered with syrup and strips of bacon on the side and glasses of orange juice and milk. "I'll have that." I pointed at the picture.

3 **to gaze at s.o.:** jdn. anblicken, jdn. anstarren. 11 **fogged:** beschlagen. 16 **menu:** Speisekarte. **to wrinkle one's nose:** die Nase rümpfen. 21 **strips of bacon:** Streifen durchwachsenen Specks.

"Okay, hon."

"Maybe you want to wash before you eat," Officer Ryan said.

"Sure." I took off the black ski jacket and went into the bathroom. In the mirror was a kid with tangled, matted hair. A flat, splotchy face smeared with dirt. Clothes that weren't much more than rags. I ran the water. It wasn't hot, but it stung my cold, stiff fingers. I had to wait a while until I could bend each finger. Then I squeezed the liquid soap into my palms and washed my face and hands. The rinse water turned a muddy light brown.

I dried my hands with the blow dryer, then turned it upside down and let the hot air blast my face. It felt good and I stayed there long after the skin was dry.

When I got back to the table, the plate of pancakes and bacon and the glasses of orange juice and milk were already there.

"I was worried that maybe you'd run away," Officer Ryan said as I slid into the booth.

"Why would I do that?" I asked.

"I don't know," she said. "Maybe you decided this was some kind of trick."

I smiled.

8 **stiff:** steif. 12 **blow dryer:** Händetrockner; Fön. 13 **to blast my face:** mir ins Gesicht blasen.

"What's so funny?" Officer Ryan asked.

"You keep saying maybe. It's my favorite word. That's what they call me. Maybe."

"All right, Maybe."

"How come you haven't asked what my real name is?" I asked.

"Would you tell me if I did?"

"Maybe."

The corners of her mouth turned up slightly, but it wasn't a happy smile. "Go ahead, have something to eat before it gets cold."

I poured syrup over the pancakes and took a bite. It was sweet and delicious. I drank some orange juice and took another bite. Officer Ryan sipped her coffee.

I only ate about half the pancakes before I started to feel too full to eat anymore.

"That's it?" Officer Ryan asked.

I nodded.

"Guess there's not much room down there," she said.

I drank a little more milk, then wiped my lips on my sleeve. I felt full and warm and sleepy. Snow was starting to fall outside. Just a few tiny white flakes here and there.

"How's the Asphalt Tribe?"

9 **corner of the mouth:** Mundwinkel. **slightly:** ein wenig. 12 **to pour:** gießen. **to take a bite:** abbeißen. 13 **delicious:** köstlich. 22 **flakes:** Flocken.

I shrugged. "They're okay."

"Who's left?"

"OG. He's the guy with the dog. Jewel. I don't know if you've met him. Maggot." I didn't mention Tears because I was pretty sure she wouldn't want me to.

"When was the last time you saw Rainbow?" Officer Ryan asked.

"That night you took us to jail," I said.

"You didn't like the Youth Housing Project?"

I shook my head.

"Too many rules?"

"Yeah."

Officer Ryan took a deep breath. "I've got bad news for you. Rainbow died."

The little flakes of snow drifted slowly down out of the gray sky. I imagined I was a white snow butterfly flapping my pure white wings as the flakes fell around me.

"They put her in a detox center, but she stayed one night and then left. Yesterday they pulled her body from the river. No visible signs of trauma so they sent her down to the ME. He'll do an autopsy."

I rubbed a spot in the frosty window and looked out at the

4 **to mention:** erwähnen, nennen. 18 **detox centre:** Entgiftungsklinik. 20 **ME:** Abk. für: Medical Examiner. 21 **autopsy:** Autopsie, Leichenuntersuchung.

falling snow. If only I'd held on to Rainbow that night … If only I hadn't let her go …

"They found her jacket on a pier nearby," Officer Ryan said. "It may have been suicide."

I was flying slowly upwards the way a butterfly does. Flap, flap through the fine light snowflakes. Up past the windows of the buildings. Past the roofs. Past the point of the Empire State Building. Up toward the clouds. There was a bright spot in the clouds above. Like an opening. A place where a glow of sunlight snuck through the gray. That's where Rainbow would be.

The black radio on Officer Ryan's belt blurped. She held it to her ear. "Ryan. Yeah. Okay. In a second." She turned off the radio. "I'm sorry, Maybe. I knew you'd want to know."

Little white flakes of snow drifting down through the gray. Flap, flap, I struggled toward the bright opening in the sky where Rainbow was waiting. But it was high, high up and far, far away, and snow was collecting on my wings, making them heavy. It was getting harder and harder to fly.

"Maybe?"

I looked across the table at Officer Ryan. She had a small dark mole right between her eyes were the eyebrows got thin and met. "You ever need help. If you ever want me to

3 **pier:** Pier, Anlegestelle. 10 **to sneak, snuck (sneaked), snuck:** kriechen, schleichen. 12 **to blurp:** piepen. 16 **to struggle:** kämpfen. 22 **mole:** Leberfleck.

help you go home, you just tell me, okay? You just come out and find me in the car or go over to the station on Avenue C and ask for me. I'll help you."

My home was with Rainbow up in the bright place in the clouds.

Officer Ryan picked up her hat. "I gotta go. Take care of yourself, okay?"

"Maybe."

I sat there for a long time. Outside the snow began to come down harder. It started to weigh down my wings and get into my eyes. Sometimes the sky was so thick with snow I couldn't see the bright spot in the clouds anymore. It stuck to my thin black antennas and legs. My white wings got too heavy to flap. I stuck them out straight the way the sea gulls did and began to glide back down in slow circles. Can't get there from here. Beneath me the dirty gray city had turned white. The roofs of buses and buildings, the sidewalks and streets. Everything was white. I landed in the snow and disappeared.

"Hon?" The waitress in the light blue sweater was standing over me. "I'm afraid I need this table. It's dinner time and other people want to eat."

I got up and pulled on the black ski jacket.

2 **station:** (Polizei)station 10 **to weigh down:** niederdrücken. 13 **antenna:** Fühler.

"Here's something to take with you." She gave me a white plastic bag. "Some bread and cheese."

"Thanks." I took the bag and went out into the snow. It was the light, fluffy kind that clung to your head and shoulders. The kind you could blow away with a strong breath. It was pretty and felt good, until I got cold again and started to shiver. I walked down the sidewalk toward the bridge, and thought about Rainbow. She loved that leather jacket and wouldn't go nowhere without it.

A big silver car came down the street in the other direction. It was covered by a thin blanket of white except for the dark green half circles where the windshield wipers swished back and forth. It slowed down, then made a U-turn. I kept walking. The car pulled next to me and I waited for the window to come down and a man inside to ask if I was hungry.

The window came down. A woman with straight blond hair looked out. "Excuse me."

I kept walking.

"Excuse me," she said again.

I didn't look at her.

She said something to someone in the car. A man's voice answered her. She turned back to me. "I'll give you a dollar if you'll look at a photograph of someone we're looking for."

4 **to cling to, clung, clung:** sich heften an. 13 **to make a U-turn:** eine Kehrtwendung machen. 14 **the car pulled next to me:** das Auto hielt neben mir. 16 **straight:** gerade.

I stopped. The car stopped. The woman held out a sheet of pictures and a dollar. The sheet was big and had half a dozen photos on it. She was barely able to get it through the window. It was still snowing and the white flakes got on the woman's arms and hair.

I took the dollar and stuffed it into my pocket. Then I looked at the photos. There was a boy with short hair wearing a white shirt and white shorts and holding a tennis racket. In another photo he was wearing khaki shorts and a blue sweatshirt and standing on a wooden dock with a sailboat behind him. Then he was in a group shot with another boy and a girl with long blond hair and a smiling man and woman. I looked at the woman in the car. It was her. She looked up at me with hopeful, pleading eyes.

"Do you know him?" she asked. "Have you seen him?"

I nodded.

1 **sheet:** Blatt; Bogen. 3 **barely:** kaum. 8 **tennis racket:** Tennisschläger. 11 **group shot:** Gruppenbild. 14 **pleading:** flehend.

TWENTY-TWO

"You don't have to come home," said the man in the tan sheepskin coat. "We just want to know that you're all right."

The man had silver hair and a deep tan. His coat had a white fur collar and more fur at the ends of the sleeves. The blond woman stood beside him wearing a dark blue coat with some sort of design on it. She was also tan. The silver car had green and white Colorado license plates.

Inside the blue tarp OG coughed. In his arms, Pest barked. Tears sat with the dirty orange sleeping bag draped over her shoulders. Jewel had gotten up and was running his fingers along the top of the silver car, making designs in the light snow. The man in the sheepskin coat kept looking at him as if he was worried Jewel would do something bad to the car. Maggot lit a cigarette he rolled himself. He inhaled and exhaled. His breath and the smoke came out in a white-gray cloud.

8 **tan sheepskin coat:** hellbrauner Mantel aus Schafsleder. 11 **deep tan:** tief gebräunte Haut. 15 **licence plates:** Autokennzeichen. 22 **to inhale:** inhalieren, einatmen. 23 **to exhale:** ausatmen.

"I don't want your help," he said.

"We understand that, Stuart," said the woman.

"My name's not Stuart. It's Maggot."

"All right," the woman said.

"Say it," Maggot said.

"Mag-gut." The woman seemed to choke on the name.

"Mercedes?" Jewel asked.

"Uh, no, it's a Lexus," answered the man.

"Oh, yes, of course," Jewel said. "Mother and father had them in matching blue. And a Rolls. And the Ferrari."

The man and woman scowled. The woman turned back to Maggot. "We want to make sure you don't get sick or hurt. It's fine if you want to stay here in New York. We can help you find a place to live."

"I'm okay right here," Maggot said.

The man and woman looked at the snow-covered garbage strewn around our little camp. The empty bottles, the charred, half-burned wood sticking out of the blackened garbage can. OG had a coughing fit that left him doubled over. The woman winced.

"At least let us take you to a doctor and have you examined." Her voice started to crack and her eyes got watery.

"Suppose we take you and your friends out to dinner," the man said. "So we know you'll get a good meal."

6 **to choke on s.th.:** sich an etw. verschlucken, ersticken. 11 **to scowl:** ein finsteres Gesicht machen. 16 **snow-covered:** mit Schnee bedeckt. 17 **strewn:** verstreut. 18 **charred:** verkohlt. 19 **to double over:** sich krümmen. 22 **to crack:** brechen.

"How fun," Jewel said. "We could go to the *Four Seasons*. That's my favorite. You can all be my guests. I have my own table, you know. It's right next to John F. Kennedy Junior's table."

"John F. Kennedy is dead, you freak," Maggot snapped irritably.

"We're all dead." OG swung his arm around. "What's the difference between this and being dead?"

Maggot's mother took a tissue out of her pocket and dabbed her eyes. His father cleared his throat. "Is there someplace nearby where we can eat?"

Maggot took another drag on his cigarette. He looked at OG and me and Jewel and Tears. Then he got up. "I'll go to dinner with you," he said. "We'll bring food back for them later."

"Escargot for me, darling!" Jewel said.

5 **irritably** (adv.): gereizt. 10 **to dab one's eyes:** sich die Augen tupfen. **to clear one's throat:** sich räuspern. 12 **to take another drag:** noch einen Zug nehmen. 16 **Escargot:** Weinbergschnecke.

TWENTY-THREE

It got dark and colder. Maggot never came back. Inside the tarp OG crawled into his nest with Pest. Jewel rocked back and forth and talked to himself. I thought about Rainbow leaving her jacket on the pier.

"Were those really Maggot's parents?" Tears asked.

"I think so," I said.

OG had a coughing fit. When the breeze blew outside, the newspapers and bags rustled like dry leaves.

"Didn't he say his parents were dead?" asked Tears.

OG coughed and spit out a glob of red. "Just a postcard punk."

"What's that?" Tears asked.

"Kid who pretends," I said. "They act like they're homeless, but they ain't. They send postcards home to let their family know they're okay."

"I never saw Maggot send a postcard," Tears said.

"It's the idea of it," said OG. "Maybe he called collect once in a while. But he left enough clues for his parents to come all the way from Colorado to find him."

17 **glob:** Klümpchen. 25 **clue:** Anhaltspunkt, Hinweis.

"Aspen is so déclassé," Jewel said. "Just yuppies and old movie stars. It's all about Whistler now. Helicopter skiing. Virgin powder and an endless vertical drop."

"What's virgin powder?" Tears asked.

"They sprinkle it on you and you become a virgin again," Jewel said. "That's what boys really want, you know. Once you give it away you're just Kleenex. Use you once and throw you away. There are other ways to satisfy boys. Hold on to what's precious, my dear."

Tears frowned. I shook my head to show she shouldn't take Jewel too seriously.

Tears got up.

"Where are you going?" I asked.

"To find a warm place to spend the night. I can't take this nomore."

"You sure?" I asked. "I could come with you."

Tears stood for a while, staring at the traffic.

"What about the Youth Housing Project?" I asked.

Tears didn't answer. She walked away into the dark.

OG coughed all night. I pictured Rainbow floating face

1 **Aspen:** Wintersportort in Colorado. **déclassé:** heruntergekommen. 2 **it's all about:** es dreht sich alles um. **Whistler:** Wintersportort. 3 **Virgin powder:** jungfräuliches Pulver (d.h. jungfräulicher Pulverschnee). **vertical drop:** steile Abfahrtspiste. 5 **to sprinkle:** sprenkeln, streuen. 9 **hold on to what's precious:** bewahre das, was kostbar ist. 20 **to picture:** sich vorstellen. **face down:** mit dem Gesicht nach unten.

down in the river, her blond hair aswirl in the dirty green water. I thought about 2Moro half naked and strangled in the park, and Country Club's dull gray eyes staring up at the clouds. Officer Johnson was right. Nobody survived on the street for long. There was nothing fun or cool about being cold and dirty and sick. Nothing glamorous about begging or being hungry or sleeping in a nest of garbage. I thought about those smooth clean sheets and the soft warm pillow at the Youth Housing Project.

Maggot always said living on the street was a choice.

But it wasn't.

It was when you ran out of choices.

1 **aswirl:** verwirbelt. 6 **glamorous:** großartig, reizvoll. 12 **to run out of choices:** keine andere Wahl mehr haben.

TWENTY-FOUR

It was warmer in the morning. The brown ice in the bottom of the squeegee bucket floated in a small ring of dirty water. I stood outside the library window until Anthony saw me. He came to the front door. "Hi, how are you?"

"Okay."

"You made it through the cold snap," he said. "I was worried about you. They say it's going to be in the forties and fifties for the rest of the week. That should be a lot better."

"I never thanked you for the sweater."

"That's all right."

"I lost it."

"Oh, well. It was old anyway. Where's Nikki?"

"Who?"

"Your friend who used the phone the other day."

"Oh, Tears. She's around."

Anthony gave me a funny look.

13 **cold snap:** Kältewelle. 14 **in the forties and fifties:** zwischen 40 und 60 Grad Fahrenheit (ca. 5 bis 15 Grad Celsius). 22 **She's around:** sie ist irgendwo hier in der Gegend.

"That's why I'm here," I said.

"Is something wrong?"

"I don't know. Yeah, I guess."

"Is she in trouble?"

"Not yet, but she will be soon," I said.

"And you want to help her before it's too late?"

I nodded.

"Let's go into my office," Anthony said, holding the door for me. "And don't worry about Bobby."

I followed him through the library and down the hall to his office. Anthony sat down at his desk. "Want some jelly beans?"

I held my hands out and he poured some in. The flavors were like bright colors in my mouth.

"What kind of help does she need?" Anthony asked.

"She needs to get out of here and go home, but she thinks her mom don't want her."

"Why?"

I told him about how Tears' mom refused to believe that her stepfather abused Tears. "The thing is, she has grandparents, but she thinks she can't bother them because her grandfather has this disease and her grandmother needs to take care of him."

13 **flavor:** Geschmack. 19 **to refuse:** sich weigern. 20 **to abuse:** (sexuell) missbrauchen. 22 **disease:** Krankheit.

"Do you know what the disease is?"

"It makes you shake all over."

"Parkinson's," Anthony said. "They have medicines now to help control that. Of course, it depends on how severe the case is. How old is Nikki?"

"Twelve or thirteen."

Anthony winced. "Okay, let's say she's twelve, and we guess that her mom is in her mid- to late thirties. That could mean the grandparents are in their sixties, which is still relatively young. I think they would at least want to know where Nikki is. Do you want me to help find her grandparents?"

"Yeah. Like, you know, on the computer."

"Any idea where she's from?"

"A place called Hundred."

"Hundred?" Anthony frowned.

"Something like that."

"Do you know the state?"

I tried to remember. I knew Tears told me. "I think it's pretty far away."

Anthony wrote something down on a pad of paper. "Well, I'll see what I can do. If I find out anything, where can I find you?"

"I'll come back," I said.

4 **severe:** ernst, schwer. 7 **to wince:** zusammenzucken. 20 **pad of paper:** Notizblock.

TWENTY-FIVE

Lightning, aka Pest. *Born in Danbury, Connecticut, breeding center. Purchased in a mall pet shop for Christmas. Considered cute for a few months, but chewed shoes and wasn't completely housebroken. "Lost" in a park near Greenwich, Connecticut. Later turned up in New York City. Adopted by OG. Dead at 14 months. Cause of death: malnutrition.*

I went back to the bridge, hoping Tears would be there. The blue tarp lay among newspapers, rags, beer cans and liquor bottles. The garbage can, charred black from the fires, stood empty and cold.

Jewel was sitting and rocking with his eyes closed, humming to himself. I thought I heard a rustling sound come from a pile of papers, rags, and bags. It looked like windblown garbage trapped against the base of the bridge. But the heap

9 **breeding centre:** Aufzuchtzentrum. **to purchase:** erwerben. **pet shop:** Tierhandlung. 10 **to consider:** ansehen, betrachten (als). **cute:** süß. 11 **to chew:** (herum)kauen. **housebroken:** stubenrein. 14 **malnutrition:** Unterernährung.

of garbage moved and I thought I heard a moan. I stepped closer. A smell began to invade my nostrils. At first it was just faint. But the closer I got the stronger it grew. I had an awful *what if* thought. The kind of thought you didn't want to know the answer to, but once you thought it you knew it would haunt you until you did.

Holding my breath I stepped closer and began to brush away the garbage. Some of it was tangled in long light brown hair. Each time my hand pushed away more garbage the smell got stronger. It wasn't body odor or rotted food or poo smell. It was something else. Something worse.

And there it was. The side of a face, caked with grime and scabs. An ear with a round plastic plug stretching out the earlobe and a raw red sore inside. A closed eye crusted with dirt and dried mucous. A nose, and cracked, scabbed lips. It was OG. I reached down and touched the side of his face. The skin was cool, but not cold. Under my fingertip I could feel the pulse in his neck.

"OG?" I said.

He didn't answer or even act like he heard me.

I turned to Jewel, who was still rocking back and forth with his eyes closed. "Wake up, Jewel. OG's really sick. We better get help."

1 **moan:** Stöhnen. 2 **to invade my nostrils:** mir in die Nase zu steigen. 3 **faint:** schwach. 6 **to haunt:** verfolgen. 11 **poo:** Kacke. 15 **mucous:** Schleim.

"The help is downstairs," Jewel answered. "You may ring for them." He kept rocking.

I brushed some more garbage away from OG's nose and mouth so that he could breathe. The smell kept getting worse. I moved another piece of newspaper away from his face. Under the paper was something brown and furry – the tip of one of Pest's ears.

I went across the street and begged a man with a cell phone to call 911. The police and an EMS truck came. The EMS people took away OG on a stretcher and Pest in a black bag. The police took Jewel in their car. He told them he had to get to the airport to catch a flight to Rio de Janeiro.

"There's no one left, Maybe."

I turned around. It was Officer Ryan. She was wearing her heavy blue coat, unzipped.

There was Tears, I thought. Or was there? She was gone. And when you went where she went you sometimes didn't come back.

"You gonna stay here alone?"

I shook my head. I didn't know where I was going, but I wasn't staying there.

"Tell you what. I got about three hours left on my shift. Just before it ends I'm gonna come back. If you're still here,

9 **911:** Notrufnummer. 10 **stretcher:** Tragbahre. 15 **unzipped:** mit offenem Reißverschluss. 22 **tell you what:** ich mach dir einen Vorschlag.

maybe you'll let me take you somewhere where you can spend the night."

"Maybe."

TWENTY-SIX

I went to the park and looked for Tears. She wasn't there, but Lost and his friends were.

"You seen Maggot?" Lost asked when he saw me.

"I think he went home," I said.

"Home?" Lost made a face. "What do you mean?"

"I mean home, like where he came from."

"How?"

"His parents picked him up in their car."

"Man." Lost shook his head in disbelief. "He said his parents were dead."

I almost told him about Rainbow. But then I didn't. "You seen Tears?" I asked.

"Who?"

"My friend with the short black hair."

"I seen her last night," said the guy with the long light brown dreadlocks. "Cruising the tunnel."

I walked over to Lincoln Tunnel. Most of the kids who

12 **to make a face:** das Gesicht verziehen. 15 **to pick up:** abholen. 16 **in disbelief:** ungläubig. 23 **to cruise:** sich herumtreiben.

"worked" there waited until dark. But a few – the really desperate ones – sometimes tried during the day. Maybe Tears would be there. I didn't know how desperate she was. I covered most of the streets around the tunnel but couldn't find her. Then I started to feel hungry and decided to go to St. Marks church for some food. But the line outside the church was long again. I knew if I went over to the Youth Housing Project I could get some food, but they had a rule that you weren't allowed to leave the house after dinner. That meant I wouldn't be able to look for Tears later.

So I stood on line with the homeless people. They were mostly men and mostly older. A lot older. Wrinkled and gray-haired and bad smelling. Me and my friends got yucky and smelled bad, too. But that was different. This was temporary for us. Something was bound to change. We weren't going to wind up old and smelly and wrinkled like these bums.

Why?

I used to think it was because something unexpected was going to happen first. Jewel would be "discovered" and get rich, and all of us would live with him in his mansion. Or some rich guy would fall in love with Rainbow and take us away to someplace nice. Or somehow we'd just keep living on the street but never get old or sick.

1 **the really desperate ones:** die ganz Verzweifelten. 13 **yucky:** schmutzig. 14 **temporary:** vorübergehend. 15 **to be bound to change:** sich bestimmt ändern werden. 16 **to wind up:** enden. 17 **bum:** Penner. 21 **mansion:** Villa. 23 **someplace nice:** irgendein schöner Ort.

Now I knew that wasn't the reason we wouldn't wind up like wrinkled, stinky bums.

The real reason was because we were going to die first.

Country Club, 2Moro, and Rainbow were dead. OG was close to dead. Maybe Jewel was as good as dead.

And maybe you really can't live on the streets.

You can only die there.

I waited on the church line. Dinner was a ham and cheese sandwich on white bread, a paper cup of chicken noodle soup, and an apple. I ate fast and then went back to look for Tears.

It got dark and I didn't find her. Then I got tired and went to sleep in a doorway.

In the morning I went to the library. Anthony was holding the front door open for me. He must have seen me through the windows. "I found Nikki's grandparents," he said, sounding excited. "There's only one place called Hundred and it's in West Virginia. I called the public library and spoke to one of the librarians. I told her I was looking for a couple, probably in their sixties. The husband had Parkinson's Disease and they had a granddaughter named Nikki who'd run away. The librarian called back two days later and said she'd found the grandparents. Their last name is

8 **church line:** Schlange vor der Kirche. **ham:** Schinken. 13 **doorway:** Hauseingang.

Frimer and they're beside themselves with worry. The librarian says they call all the time to find out if she's heard anything more about Nikki."

So somebody did love Tears. Someone worried about her.

"Do you know where she is?" Anthony asked.

I shook my head. "I been looking."

"I'll help you," Anthony said.

"Why?"

Anthony's eyebrows rose in surprise. "Because she should go home. She shouldn't stay on the street."

"Why do you care?" I asked again.

"I ... I just do. You're all so young. You don't know how lucky you are. When you get to be older all you'll wish for is more time. It's the most valuable thing there is, and I hate to see anyone throw it away."

He sounded sincere. I couldn't really understand people like him. Or maybe I could.

Because we were alike. We looked strange and that made us different. It set us apart. Was he lonely? Did helping Tears and me give him something to do?

"What do you think about that," Anthony said. "I take the afternoon off and we go and look for Nikki together."

I thought about it for a moment. "We should wait until later."

1 **beside themselves with worry:** außer sich vor Sorge. 14 **valuable:** wertvoll. 18 **alike:** ähnlich. 21 **to take the afternoon off:** sich für den Nachmittag freinehmen.

"Okay, the library's open late tonight," Anthony said. "I'll be here until nine. What will you do between now and then?"

"I'll keep looking," I said. "I'll come back here later."

TWENTY-SEVEN

I looked for Tears in the park again. It was dark, and hard to see who was sleeping on the grass under blankets or in sleeping bags. They all looked like lumps of clay. I climbed over the iron fence and walked through the grassy area inside. Some of the lumps looked too big to be Tears, and it was too dark to tell if Tears was one of the smaller lumps. After a while I climbed back over the fence and checked in front of the *Good Life* and the bakery. No sign of her. Then I headed toward the tunnel. She had to be somewhere around there.

"Hey," a voice said.

A police car pulled up. Officer Johnson leaned out the window. "What are you up to again?"

"I'm just looking for my friend."

"Sure you are." Johnson smirked. "Any friend you can find."

10 **lumps of clay:** Lehmklumpen. 11 **iron fence:** Eisenzaun. 15 **no sign of her:** keine Spur von ihr. 20 **What are you up to again?:** Was führst du jetzt schon wieder im Schilde? 22 **sure you are:** (ironisch) ja, klar.

"No, just one," I said. "She's kind of short, with short black hair and big eyes."

Officer Johnson said something to the cop driving the car, then turned to me. "Some kid got run over by a truck a couple of hours ago. Driver said she simply wandered out into the middle of traffic. He hit the brakes but there was nothing he could do."

I felt my heart stop cold. "Is … she okay?"

Johnson shook his head. "It don't look good."

I started to run.

"You kids never listen," Officer Johnson yelled behind me. "I told ya a hundred times. Get off the damn street. But ya never listen."

I ran down the dark sidewalk toward the library. I had to tell Anthony.

I bounded up the stairs, through the front door and past that metal detector thing. One of the ID women behind the front counter yelled, "Hey!" I ignored her and went to the computer tables. People were sitting at almost every computer, but Anthony wasn't there. I didn't understand. He said he worked late tonight.

"Hey, you!" It was Bobby. He must've heard the ID woman's shout. "What do you want?"

4 **to get run over:** überfahren werden. **truck:** LKW. 12 **ya:** *you*. 16 **to bound up:** heraufspringen. 17 **ID women:** hier: Büchereiangestellte. 18 **front counter:** Kundenschalter im Eingangsbereich.

The people at the computers stopped what they were doing and watched Bobby and me circle the table.

"Anthony said the library is open to the public and anyone can use it," I said.

"Yeah, they can use it," Bobby said. "Not run around and make messes."

"I didn't make no mess," I said. "I came to see Anthony."

"He ain't here."

"Yes, he is." It was Anthony, coming from the back. He must've seen that I was breathing hard and looked scared. "What's wrong?"

"Tears got hit by a truck."

"Wait here. I'll be right back." Anthony hurried toward his office. Bobby kept his eye on me. Like I was a wild animal that escaped from its cage.

A few moments later Anthony came back, pulling on his brown coat and tying his scarf. "Let's go."

We left the library. "Which hospital is she in?" Anthony asked.

"I don't know."

"They didn't tell you?"

"All I know is what Officer Johnson said. She was hit by a truck and it looked bad."

2 **to circle the table:** den Tisch umkreisen. 6 **to make messes:** Unordnung machen. 15 **to escape from a cage:** aus einem Käfig ausbrechen. 17 **to tie one's scarf:** sich den Schal binden.

Anthony stopped on the sidewalk, watching the headlights of the cars on the street. "Let's go to the police station. They'll know."

Anthony walked ahead taking long strides, and I had to walk real fast to keep up with him. We turned a corner and saw the station house ahead. It was a low, square brick building with flagpoles jutting out from the second floor. The sidewalk in front of the station was brightly lit, and a row of police cars was parked at an angle in the street. Anthony pushed through the glass doors and I followed him into an open lobby filled with wooden benches and lined with doors. People sat on the benches. Women with babies sucking on pacifiers. Silent old men. A group of students with backpacks, huddled close together and talking.

Anthony went to a scuffed Plexiglas window with small holes punched through it. On the other side a police officer sat at a counter writing on a pad.

"Excuse me," Anthony said. "We're trying to find out about a young woman who was hit by a truck a few hours ago."

"What do you want to know?" the officer asked.

"Is she okay? Where is she?"

"Who are you?"

"Friends," Anthony said.

4 **to take long strides:** große Schritte machen 7 **flagpole:** Fahnenstange. **to jut out:** hinausragen. 11 **lined with doors:** mit vielen Türen. 13 **pacifier:** Schnuller. 15 **scuffed:** verschrammt.

The police officer's eyebrows rose slightly. He glanced at me and then back at Anthony. "Wait here." He got up and disappeared through a door in the back. After a while the door opened and a skinny man wearing a brown suit came out. His eyes fixed on Anthony. "You asking about the kid who was hit by the truck?"

Anthony nodded and the man in the brown suit gestured for him to come closer. I started to go with him, but Anthony put his hand on my shoulder. "Wait here," he said.

Anthony went to the door. The man in the brown suit spoke quietly. Anthony listened and then said something I couldn't hear. The man in the brown suit took out a pad of paper and a pen and wrote something down. Then he shook Anthony's hand and went back inside. Anthony walked slowly toward me. His shoulders were hunched over and he was staring at the floor.

"Let's sit down," he said.

"No." I knew what he was going to say. But it couldn't be true. It just couldn't. Not after Country Club and 2Moro and Rainbow.

Anthony hung his head. "She wasn't carrying any ID. They didn't know who she was. I gave him her name and the town she comes from. He's going to call her mom. Someone

4 **suit:** Anzug. 7 **gestured for him to come closer:** winkte ihn zu sich. 15 **hunched over:** gebeugt.

from her family has to come here to make a positive identification."

So that was it. My friends were all gone. There was no more Asphalt Tribe. The only people in the world that I cared about, and the only people who cared about me. A month ago we were all together. Now there was no one left. Only me. Tears flooded my eyes. That wet wind started to blow. Didn't even occur to me to try and fight it. I stood there and cried.

I felt a pair of arms go around me. Felt the soft, fuzzy cloth of Anthony's brown coat against my face. Yes, he was one of the nice ones. But sooner or later he'd leave, too. Everyone left.

"Come on, Maybe, let's go." I let him guide me out of the police station and back out into the cold dark.

"Hungry?" Anthony asked.

I shook my head and tasted the dirty tears that ran down into the corners of my mouth.

"No, I didn't think you would be," Anthony said. "Sorry, it was a dumb question."

"It's okay," I said with a sniff.

We started to walk. I don't think either of us knew where we were going.

1 **to make a positive identification:** jdn. identifizieren. 10 **cloth:** Stoff.
20 **dumb:** dumm.

"Perhaps the best way to look at this is that you're lucky," Anthony said. "For some reason you've been spared. You alone have been given another chance. It's almost as if someone's looking out for you, Maybe."

Looking out for me? I looked upward. It was dark, but the lights of the city lit the low clouds in the sky above. Could it be? It was hard to believe. But maybe. You never knew. We walked for a while. Anthony didn't say nothing more. We turned a corner.

"What's this?" Anthony asked.

A long line of people stood on the sidewalk across the street. They were all dressed up, smoking and talking. "They're waiting to get into a club."

"Where?" Anthony looked down the street.

"Around the next corner. It's called *The Cradle*."

"It must be huge to hold all these people."

"No, because half of them won't get in."

Anthony and I walked along the sidewalk on the other side of the street from the crowd.

"I'm going to try very hard not to say all the obvious things you'd expect from a middle-aged librarian," Anthony said as he stared at the costumes and make-up. "I'm not going to ask which ones are male and which are female. I'm not

2 **you've been spared:** du bist verschont geblieben. 4 **looking out for:** beschützen. 12 **dressed up:** herausgeputzt. 16 **it must be huge to hold all these people:** es muss riesig sein, dass all die Leute da reinpassen.

going to ask how they can manage to go out at midnight and still get up for work in the morning. I'm not going to ask why some of them look so young or why –"

I didn't hear the rest because I'd spotted a ghost.

4 **to spot:** sehen, entdecken. **ghost:** Geist, Gespenst.

TWENTY-EIGHT

"Tears?" I couldn't believe what I was seeing, but I was sure it was her. I practically skipped across the street.

Tears looked in my direction and her eyes got too big for her head. She was wearing a black leather jacket, a tight black skirt, and long black boots. Someone made her up to look more like 21 than 12.

"I can't believe you're alive!" I gushed. "We thought you got run over by a truck!"

I thought she would smile or laugh, but she just frowned. I slowed down, then stopped on the sidewalk near her and lowered my voice. "What is it? What's wrong?"

"Go away," she whispered.

"Why?"

"He's gonna come back and see you and he'll be really mad."

"Who? Jack?"

9 **to skip:** springen, hüpfen. 14 **to gush:** herausplatzen. 18 **to lower one's voice:** die Stimme senken.

"Who's Jack?"

"That guy we met here the last time," I said.

"Not him. Someone else."

I looked at her more closely. Her hair had a freshly washed sheen and her make-up didn't have a single smear. Her jacket was so new you could smell the leather.

"And my name ain't Tears nomore," she said. "It's Lacey."

I felt a hand close around my arm and spin me around. It was the short, stocky man with the shaved head and the diamond earrings. The one who pushed me into the bar the last time I was at *The Cradle*. His long black leather coat hung open and he was wearing a black T-shirt underneath.

"What do you want?"

"I'm her friend," I said.

"She don't got no friends unless I say so." I felt his hand tighten on my arm, just like the last time. I wanted to tell him he needed a new act.

"Nikki!" someone shouted. "Nikki!" It was Anthony. He rushed up to Tears and hugged her. "Oh, honey, I'm so happy I found you! What are you doing here? Your mom and I have been so worried. We thought we'd never see you again."

The short man with the diamond earrings let go of my arm. "Now what? Who are you?"

5 **sheen:** Glanz. 8 **to spin around:** herumdrehen, herumschleudern. 9 **stocky:** stämmig. 17 **he needed a new act:** er sollte sich mal was Neues ausdenken. 19 **to rush up to s.o.:** auf jdn. zustürzen.

"I'm her father," Anthony said. "Who are you?"

The short bald man's forehead bunched up with confusion. "You can't be her father."

"Why not?" Anthony asked loudly. "What are you? Some kind of racist?"

The other people on line started to stare.

"Keep it down," said the guy.

"Her name is Nikki Frimer and she comes from West Virginia and I am her father." Anthony hugged Tears again. I had to give him credit for playing the part so well. "Nikki, hon, I know we've had our differences, but your mom and I got so scared when you ran away. I promise we'll be more open-minded from now on. You don't even have to live with us if you don't want to. I spoke to Grammy. She said Grandpa David is taking a new medicine and his Parkinson's disease is much better. She said it would be no problem if you wanted to stay with them."

Tears's eyes went about as wide as they could. She looked at me and I mouthed the words, "It's true."

"Maybe she don't want to go back to West Virginia," said the man with the shaved head. "Maybe she want to stay here."

"Listen, I don't know who you are, but my daughter hap-

2 **to bunch up:** sich in Falten legen. **with confusion:** vor Verwirrung. 7 **Keep it down:** macht nicht so einen Krach. 10 **to give s.o. credit for s.th.:** jnd. etw. hoch anrechnen. **part:** Rolle. 13 **open-minded:** aufgeschlossen. 23 **My daughter happens to be thirteen years old:** Meine Tochter ist zufälligerweise erst dreizehn Jahre alt.

pens to be thirteen years old," Anthony said angrily. "Do you know what happens to men who take advantage of young girls?" He reached into his pocket and pulled out a cell phone. "Perhaps you'd like to have the police explain it to you."

The man with the shaved head quickly raised his hands. "Wait a minute. Wait a minute. Okay, I see where you come from."

"And I see where you're going." Anthony pointed his cell phone down the street. "And if I were you, I'd get going very fast."

2 **to take advantage of s.o.:** jnd. ausnützen. 10 **I'd get going:** ich würde mich auf die Beine machen.

TWENTY-NINE

We stayed in Anthony's apartment that night. In his living room a TV sat in a black cabinet against the wall across from a blue couch and a coffee table. The walls were lined with bookshelves and framed paintings. Deep yellow curtains hung over the windows. Hard to remember the last time I'd been in a room with curtains. Everything was neat and clean.

"You wait here," Anthony said, and went down the hall.

We waited. Tears looked at something on one of the bookshelves. It was a small blue stone turtle with sparkling red eyes. The way the eye stones shimmered made me think that they might be valuable. Tears picked it up and studied it more closely. She gave me a questioning look.

"Don't," I said.

"Why not?"

"Because he's being nice to us."

9 **cabinet:** Schrank. 10 **the walls were lined with bookshelves:** an den Wänden standen lauter Bücherregale. 17 **turtle:** Schildkröte. **sparkling:** funkelnd.

"For now," Tears said. "Just wait."

"No, I think maybe he's different."

She put the turtle down just as Anthony came back with two thick, fluffy light blue towels. "Here. These towels are for your shower."

Tears gave me an uncertain look. I wasn't sure I felt like taking a shower, but I had the feeling that for Anthony it was the price of admission. I remembered he was kind of a clean freak, always washing his hands and even wiping the phone after Tears used it. Tears was probably worried that if we took turns in the bathroom it would mean one of us would be alone with Anthony when the other was showering.

"Come on," I said. "We'll take a shower together."

We went into the bathroom and locked the door. The bathroom was small and lined with green tiles. There was hardly enough room for us to undress without our elbows banging into each other. I reached over the tub and started the shower. Warm steam filled the bathroom. "Come on, Tears," I said.

We got into the shower and began to wash. The water felt soothing and we lathered shampoo into our hair and took turns rinsing it out. My hair was still a tangle of knots, but at least it would be clean. I washed off the dirt and Tears

8 **price of admission:** Eintrittspreis. 16 **to bang:** stoßen. 21 **soothing:** entspannend. **to lather:** einschäumen, einreiben. 22 **to rinse:** spülen **tangle of knots:** Gewirr von Knoten.

washed off her make-up and then we weren't street kids anymore. Well, at least we didn't look it.

The hot water felt so good that we stayed until our fingers got wrinkly. Finally we got out and dried ourselves with these soft, fluffy towels.

"Now what?" Tears asked.

"Do this." I wrapped the towel around me and tucked it so it wouldn't come loose. Then we went back to the living room. Anthony had pushed the coffee table out of the way and pulled a folding bed out of the couch.

"Is this where you want us to sleep?" I asked.

"No," he answered. "I'll sleep here. You two sleep in the bedroom. That bed's bigger and softer than this."

Tears and me went back down the hall to the bedroom. Inside, the bed had been turned down. Two folded white T-shirts lay on the pale red blanket.

Tears held one up. "What are these for?"

"He probably left them for us to sleep in," I said.

Tears pulled the T-shirt on over her head, then locked the bedroom door. I didn't argue. Even with Anthony you couldn't be a hundred percent sure. That's the way it was with grown-ups. You just never knew for sure. I crawled into the bed and Tears got in on the other side. My head

6 **Now what?:** was jetzt? 7 **to tuck:** feststecken. 10 **folding bed:** Klappbett. 20 **to argue:** Einwände vorbringen. 22 **to crawl:** kriechen, krabbeln.

sank into the pillow, and my body settled into the mattress. The sheets were soft and smooth.

The room was lit by a small lamp on the night table on Tears's side of the bed.

"Night, Maybe." She yawned and started to reach for the lamp.

"Don't," I said.

"You're afraid?"

"Afraid I'll fall asleep," I said. The bed felt so good, so warm and comfortable. This was the second time in a week that I slept in a real bed. In my head I could hear Maggot complaining that soft, warm beds were just too middleclass for him. What a joke. It made me a little angry to remember his beautifully dressed parents and that expensive car. He was the most middleclass of all. Just a postcard punk taking a walk on the wild side with his fake talk about class war and revolution. Well, right now I could care less. All I knew was it felt good between those sheets.

12 **to complain:** sich beschweren. **too middleclass:** zu spießig. 15 **to take a walk on the wild side:** ein Abenteuer erleben. 16 **fake talk:** leeres Gerede.

THIRTY

The next morning Anthony got us up early and took us to a diner for breakfast, but he left soon, saying he'd be right back. A while passed and I was beginning to wonder if he'd ever come back when he drove up in a rented car. It took eight hours to drive to Hundred, West Virginia, and we listened to the radio the whole way. Tears and me sat in the back seat and told Anthony when to change the station. I don't think we heard a single song Anthony liked; he said he was into opera, and you better believe we didn't listen to none of *that* crap.

Thanks to this rental car thing called a GPS, Anthony drove right to the trailer park where Nikki's grandparents lived. Inside were some of the biggest trailers I ever seen. A few looked as big as houses and had concrete driveways and aboveground pools. Some had bird feeders and basketball hoops, and even though it was January you could see where

11 **rented car:** Mietwagen. 14 **to change the station:** den Sender wechseln. 18 **GPS** *(Global Positioning System)*: Navigationssystem. 19 **trailer park:** Wohnwagenplatz. 22 **aboveground pool:** oberirdischer (nicht versenkter) Swimmingpool. **bird feeder:** Vogelhäuschen. **basketball hoop:** Basketballring.

the gardens and flowerbeds were. A few of the lawns still had plastic reindeers or Nativity scenes from Christmas.

Anthony parked the car in a driveway next to a white trailer with green trim and a red door. When we got out of the car, birds burst from a brown wooden bird feeder on a pole next to the driveway. Some small bushes in the yard were covered with burlap, and a wind chime near the front door made soft tinkling sounds.

The door opened and a small woman with rosy cheeks and gray hair hurried out. "Nikki!" she cried.

We still sat in the car. Tears turned to me with those round eyes she made whenever she was surprised or scared. We'd had fun in the car, but now all of a sudden she looked nervous.

"Go on," I said in a low voice.

Tears pressed a finger between her lips and began to gnaw on the nail.

"She's your grandma," I said. "She won't bite."

Tears slowly pushed open the door. In an instant she was swallowed up in a hug by her grandmother. "Oh, Nikki, Nikki!" she cried. "We thought you were dead. A policeman called from New York and said you'd been run over by a truck."

2 **reindeer:** Rentier. **Nativity scene:** Weihnachtskrippe. 4 **trim:** Zierstreifen. 5 **to burst from:** herausschießen aus. **pole:** Pfahl. 7 **burlap:** Sackleinen. **wind chime:** vom Wind bewegtes Glockenspiel. 19 **instant:** Augenblick. 20 **swallowed up:** verschluckt.

In the front seat Anthony turned around to me. "We should give them a moment alone."

I nodded. Outside, tears were streaming down the old woman's face while she smothered her granddaughter in a bear hug.

After a while we got out of the car and Tears introduced us to her Grammy Emma, who wiped the tears from her eyes and couldn't stop thanking us for bringing her granddaughter home. It seemed like she really meant it, too. Then she invited us in. She tried to call Tears' mom to tell her Tears was okay, but there was no answer. We sat in the kitchen of the trailer. The window had white curtains and was lined with little flowerpots. Tears' Grandpa shuffled in using a cane. He was a tall, bent man with a big hooked nose.

Emma served us sugar cookies and tea and milk. She talked about the cucumbers and zucchinis and green beans she grew in her garden the previous summer, and the ribbon she won at the county fair for best strawberry-rhubarb pie. She talked about the new medicines that were making her husband feel better and shake less. She seemed really happy but tense. Tears didn't say a thing. Emma didn't ask her about New York City. She didn't talk about Tears' mom and stepfather or what Tears would do now that she was back in

4 **to smother:** (fast) erdrücken. 5 **bear hug:** ungestüme Umarmung. 13 **to shuffle:** schlurfen, schleppend gehen. 14 **cane:** Stock. **bent:** gebeugt. **hooked nose:** Hakennase. 18 **rhubarb:** Rhabarber. **pie:** Obstkuchen. 21 **tense:** angespannt.

Hundred. You could see she was trying really hard to make Tears feel comfortable, but she simply talked too much. Anthony finished his tea and I finished my milk and cookies. Almost a whole day had passed and my stomach didn't hurt once. Still, I wanted to go. The trailer didn't feel as big on the inside as it looked on the outside, and I was beginning to feel restless and penned in. Tears wrinkled her forehead and started to bite her lip. No doubt she was damned scared about being left alone with her grandparents.

"You sure you don't want to stay the night and get a fresh start in the morning?" Emma quickly asked Anthony. "We've got room."

I think she was scared that Tears was going to change her mind and want to go back with us. But also a bit scared about Tears staying there. Anthony glanced at Tears and looked like he didn't know what to say.

"It's okay, Grammy," Tears said. "It's a long way back. They should probably get going."

"You sure?" I said. "I guess we could stay."

"No." Tears shook her head. "This is something I know I have to do."

I stared at her for a moment. I don't think I ever realized how brave she was until she said that.

7 **restless:** unruhig. **penned in:** eingesperrt. 13 **to change one's mind:** die Meinung ändern. 23 **brave:** tapfer, mutig.

She and Emma walked us out to the car.

"Will I ever see you again?" Tears asked.

I had to swallow hard. Somehow I knew we probably wouldn't. I'd go back to New York and she'd stay here. We'd be too far away from each other.

I felt a pang in my chest. So this was the last time. The real end of our Asphalt Tribe. It was still hard to believe what had happened to everyone. Except I'd been there. I'd seen it. I'd ... lived through it.

Why had I lived and not 2Moro? Or Rainbow? Who knew why? Maybe life was just a matter of luck and nothing more.

Tears was waiting.

"I'll call you," I said.

She and I hugged each other, then Emma hugged me and she got all teary and said, "Thank you so much again for bringing Nikki home."

Anthony and me got into the car and backed out of the driveway. I rolled down the window and waved until Tears was out of sight. Then I turned forward and watched the road. They were gone. Tears, Rainbow, Maggot, Jewel, 2Moro, OG, Pest and Country Club. Just vanished. Two to homes where people seemed to love them, two to hospitals

3 **to swallow:** schlucken. 6 **pang:** Stich. 14 **to call:** anrufen. 22 **to vanish:** verschwinden.

or the nut house, and four to unmarked graves in places where no one would ever find them again.

"Are you happy for Tears?" Anthony asked as he drove.

"Maybe."

"You're sad?"

"It's nice to have someone who cares about you."

Anthony drove on without saying anything for a while. We passed lots of farms. Lots of bare brown fields and tall blue silos and farmhouses with gray satellite dishes on window sills.

"Maybe," he finally said. "Right now there is no one in your life who cares about you the way Emma cares about Nikki. Maybe that's something only family can give, and if you don't have family, you don't always get it. But it doesn't mean *you* can't care about you. You've had some bad breaks in life. But you can still make it."

I wasn't sure I wanted to hear that. Anyway I was thinking about something else. "Could I turn on the radio?" Anthony sighed. I guess he was imaging another eight hours of the same music we made him listen to on the way to Hundred. "Sure. Go ahead."

I pushed the buttons until I found a song. When that song ended I found another song. The music was like food to my

1 **nut house:** Irrenanstalt. 8 **bare:** kahl. 9 **satellite dish:** Satellitenschüssel. **window sill:** Fensterbank. 15 **You've had some bad breaks:** Du hast einiges durchgemacht. 22 **button:** Knopf.

ears. If I didn't like one song I could pick another station. It was so easy and so much fun. After a while I looked at Anthony. He was grinning.

"What's so funny?" I asked.

"You can't get enough of it, can you?" he said. "It's such a simple pleasure, but you're so completely absorbed in it."

"I don't usually get to pick the music," I said.

"Maybe, listen." Anthony got serious. "If you lived somewhere – I mean, practically anyplace with a roof – you could have all the music you wanted. All you need is a radio. Didn't they have music at the Youth Housing Project?"

"I guess."

"If you lived there you could have it all the time."

I turned to another song. Living there meant obeying those stupid rules about when I had to eat and sleep. Then again, at least I'd have a bed. And getting food wouldn't be a job that sometimes took all day. They'd just serve it.

It started to get dark. Anthony held the steering wheel with one hand. He yawned and covered his mouth with the other.

"You hungry?"

"Uh huh."

"I don't think we can make it all the way back to the city tonight," he said. "We should probably stop around Lan-

6 **completely absorbed:** völlig gefangen genommen. 7 **to pick:** auswählen. 14 **to obey:** gehorchen, befolgen. 16 **a job that took all day:** eine Arbeit, für die man den ganzen Tag brauchte. 17 **to serve:** bringen, servieren.

caster and have dinner and find a motel. Then finish the trip tomorrow."

"Okay."

Through the car's window. I watched the clouds in the sky turn pink, then purple, then vanish into the dark. Anthony yawned again. "Maybe?"

"Yeah?"

"You never told me your real name."

"Jesse."

Anthony smiled. "That's a nice name. So, Jesse, what do you think you'll do when we get back to New York City?"

I didn't answer. I know he was trying hard to be friendly. But what should I have said anyway? I simply didn't know. Outside it was really dark now. Very different from the city. All we saw were the car lights and the signs along the side of the highway.

"The world's big, Jesse," Anthony finally said. "There are lots of places to live, and lots of ways to live. All you have to do is find the place that's right for you."

A bright green sign high above the trees on the side of the highway said something about Lancaster. Anthony steered the car toward the ramp and started to slow down.

"Can we go to the ocean?" I asked.

5 **purple:** violett. 21 **to steer:** steuern, lenken. 22 **ramp:** Ausfahrtspur.

"What?" Anthony asked, like he thought he hadn't heard me right.

"The ocean. Can we go see it?"

"When?"

"Tomorrow?"

In the dimness of the car Anthony pressed his lips together.

"Are you serious?"

"Uh huh."

"Well, I guess we do have to go through New Jersey on the way home. Why do you want to see the ocean, Jesse?"

"I just do."

"It's the middle of the winter, Jesse. It's going to be very cold."

"So? I'm homeless, remember? I'm used to that."

We spent the night in a motel. Anthony got a room for himself and another one for me. In the morning we drove to a place called Belmar in New Jersey. It was a cold gray day and Anthony drove through the empty town to an empty parking lot. Next to the parking lot was a long wooden sidewalk with some benches, and on the other side of that was the beach, and past that were waves and the most water I ever seen.

"Now what?" Anthony asked with a puzzled grin.

6 **dimness:** Halbdunkel, Dämmerlicht. 19 **parking lot:** Parkplatz. 23 **puzzled:** verblüfft, verwundert.

"You can drive right up to the ocean?" I asked.

"Why not?"

"I don't know. I guess I thought it wasn't allowed. Can I go?"

Anthony stared through the windshield. The sky was one shade of gray. The ocean was a darker shade. The waves crashed into dull white foam on the shore. "Be my guest."

I got out of the car. A chilling wet wind blew off the ocean and right through my clothes. It smelled salty and a little fishy. I grit my teeth and crossed the wooden sidewalk to the beach. The waves crashed and sea spray flew into my face. My shoes sank into the beach, so I pulled them off and left them where it was dry. I walked to the edge where the sand turned dark with seawater. It was icy around my bare feet, but I didn't care. Like the detective had said. This wasn't like seeing it on TV. This was feeling and smelling and hearing and tasting. Not like nothing I ever imagined. Different than anyplace I'd ever been.

A big wave crashed and the suds raced up the beach and around my ankles. I felt the icy chill and my feet sank deeper in the wet sand. My teeth were chattering, but I didn't want to leave. I knew I was feeling something I never felt before. Maybe Anthony was right. There were probably a lot of dif-

6 **shade of gray:** Grauton. 7 **foam:** Schaum. **Be my guest:** nur zu. 8 **chilling:** eisig. 10 **to grit o.'s teeth:** die Zähne zusammenbeißen. 11 **spray:** Gischt, Sprühnebel. 14 **icy:** eisig.

ferent places to live. And probably a lot of ways to live, too. Maybe I should venture the one or the other. One thing I was pretty sure of now – anyplace was better than the street.

"Jesse?"

I turned around. Anthony was standing on the beach with his hands shoved deep into his pockets. "Come on," he said. "Before you get sick."

"Okay." I turned back up the beach. My feet felt numb and I couldn't stop shivering. But the funny thing was, I had a feeling I wouldn't get sick. I might even get better.

2 **to venture:** wagen; ausprobieren.

Lies mich ...

Leseprobe aus dem Ravensburger Taschenbuch 58172 »Ich knall euch ab!« von Morton Rhue

Ich habe mich hinter dem Getränketisch versteckt. Wir waren da zu dritt. Die anderen beiden waren nicht wirklich beliebt, aber immerhin gehörten sie zu denen, die sich am Rand einer Clique aufhalten und manchmal eingeladen werden mitzumachen, wenn mal richtig viel Leute gebraucht werden zu einem Spiel oder zum Tanzen oder zu einer großen Party. Die zwei haben sich vor Angst fast in die Hose gemacht. Die haben bestimmt gedacht, wenn Brendan und Gary sie finden, werden sie erschossen.

Allison Findley

Ich habe ihnen gesagt, sie sollen aufhören, an die Decke zu schießen. Dass ein Querschläger jemanden genauso gut töten könne wie ein gezielter Schuss. Und sofort hat einer der beiden die nächste Salve abgefeuert. Er wusste natürlich, dass die Querschläger ihn genauso gut wie jeden anderen treffen konnten. Offenbar war ihm das gleichgültig. Ich denke, ich kann die Stimmungen von Schülern ganz gut beurteilen. Ich kann erkennen, wenn sie eine Show abziehen und nur so tun als ob. Glauben Sie mir, diese Jungen haben keine Show abgezogen.

Dick Flanagan

Wissen Sie, was verrückt ist? Die Schule ist jetzt ungefähr zwanzig Jahre alt, und ich erinnere mich noch an die ersten Baupläne für das Gebäude und an die heftigen Diskussionen, als es um die Größe der Turnhalle ging. Da wurde unter anderem gesagt, die Halle sei zu groß, das sei die reinste Geldverschwendung. Aber wenn Sie mich fragen, warum niemand durch einen Querschläger zu Schaden gekommen ist, dann sage ich's Ihnen: weil die Turnhalle so verdammt groß ist.

Allen Curry

Ich weiß noch, wie ich mich gefragt habe, warum sie nicht von Anfang an auf uns geschossen haben. Und dann habe ich gedacht: *Nein, es geht ihnen nicht darum, uns zu töten. Die müssen erst noch irgendeine blöde Botschaft loswerden, die wir uns anhören sollen.*

Deirdre Bunson

Warum haben sie Taschenlampen und was zu essen mitgebracht? Weil sie nicht vorhatten, die anderen einfach nur so zu töten. Sie wollten sie leiden lassen. Genau so, wie diese Typen uns hatten leiden lassen.

Allison Findley

Ich habe einigermaßen breite Schultern, aber meine Arme sind eher kurz, weil ich ja nicht besonders groß bin. Außerdem sind meine Arme ziemlich dick, vom Gewichtheben. Das heißt, es ist für mich gar nicht so einfach, die Arme auf den Rücken zu kriegen. Und als sie mir die Hände auf den

Rücken fesselten, konnten sie das Band nicht richtig festziehen. Ich hatte noch ein bisschen Bewegungsspielraum.

Paul Burns

Ob ich überrascht war, als ich davon gehört habe? Ja vielleicht, ganz kurz, aber nicht wirklich. Man muss das als eine Art Folter sehen. Tagaus, tagein. Die Gesellschaft schickt dich auf die Schule, und dann wirst du von der Gesellschaft in der Schule gefoltert. Man erkennt, dass es keine Fluchtmöglichkeit gibt. Jeder bleibt nur stark bis zu einem bestimmten Punkt. Und wenn der überschritten wird, dreht man durch. Wenn Brendan und Gary nicht durchgedreht wären, wer weiß, dann wäre vielleicht jemand anders durchgedreht.

Ryan Clancy

Die erste Bombe ging hoch, als sie noch dabei waren, die Leute zu fesseln. Der Knall hörte sich an, als käme er von draußen. Als jemand fragte: »Was war das?«, sagte Brendan, das sei eine Warnung, damit wollten sie dafür sorgen, dass sie nicht gestört würden. Die Schüler waren ohnehin schon verängstigt und weinten und wimmerten. Aber diese Bombe hat ihre Angst noch um ein Vielfaches gesteigert. Das war einer der vielen Augenblicke an diesem Abend, wo ich überzeugt war, dass wir alle sterben würden.

Beth Bender

Es war furchtbar. Wir mussten auf dem Bauch in die Mitte der Turnhalle kriechen. Der Boden war staubig und wir mussten uns mit dem Gesicht da reinlegen. Dann hat einer der beiden uns bewacht, und der andere hat ein paar Mädchen befohlen, sie sollten aufstehen und sich mit dem Rücken an die Türen setzen. Hat mich nicht überrascht, dass sie dazu Mädchen genommen haben. Sie hätten sich nicht getraut, einen Jungen aufstehen zu lassen.

Deirdre Bunson

Sie sprachen darüber, was sie mit ihm machen wollten. Und zwar laut, damit es auch jeder hören konnte. Er sollte sich auf den Rücken drehen, damit sie ihn ins Knie schießen konnten. In die Kniekehle wollten sie ihn nicht schießen, weil sie nicht genau wussten, ob er davon zum Krüppel würde oder nicht. Sie wollten ihm die Kniescheibe zerschießen. Damit er auch wirklich sein Leben lang was davon hat, sagten sie.

Paul Burns

Sie hörten gar nicht auf, mich zu treten, an den Kopf, an die Arme, in die Rippen. Die Hände waren mir auf den Rücken gefesselt, und ich konnte mich nicht wehren. So was von Schmerzen habe ich nicht mal bei den schlimmsten Fouls auf dem Football-Platz erlebt. Sie wollten, dass ich mich auf den Rücken drehe, damit sie mir ins Knie schießen konnten. Aber ich hab's einfach nicht getan. Ich konnte nur an die nächste Football-Saison denken. So durfte das nicht enden. Es durfte einfach nicht.

Sam Flach

Versuchen Sie sich das mal vorzustellen: Fünfzig, sechzig Jungen und Mädchen, die mit dem Gesicht auf dem harten Boden der Turnhalle liegen, die Hände auf dem Rücken gefesselt. Alles weint und winselt und schluchzt und fleht um Gnade, bettelt, dass man sie gehen lässt. Irgendwie waren diese Typen wie Jäger, und wir waren irgendwelche Robben, und die beiden überlegten nur noch, wen von uns sie als Erstes töten sollten.

Dustin Williams

Ich bin schon mein Leben lang Jäger und Waffensammler und ich bin seit fast dreißig Jahren eingeschriebenes Mitglied der National Rifle Association und spreche mich so auch öffentlich für das Recht der Amerikaner auf Waffenbesitz aus. Aber wenn ich daran denke, dass diese Jungen meine Waffen benutzt haben. Dass es meine Munition war, die sie abgefeuert haben … Natürlich kann man sagen, wenn sie die Waffen nicht mir gestohlen hätten, hätten sie sie jemand anderem gestohlen, aber so war's nun mal nicht. Diese Waffen haben mir gehört. Und jetzt muss ich damit leben.

Jack Phillips

Es war schwierig, die beiden gleichzeitig im Auge zu behalten, aber jedes Mal wenn ich dachte, sie sehen nicht hin, habe ich versucht, meine Fesseln zu lockern. Ich war mir ziemlich sicher, dass ich mich davon befreien konnte.

Paul Burns

Die Schusswunde hat verteufelt wehgetan. Ich habe die ganze Zeit damit gerechnet, ohnmächtig zu werden oder Blut im Mund zu schmecken, aber seltsamerweise habe ich mich, von den Schmerzen einmal abgesehen, ganz gut gefühlt.

Allen Curry

Man konnte ja nicht viel sehen. Wenn man den Kopf hochgehoben und sich umgeschaut hat, hat man ziemlich bald einen Krampf in den Nackenmuskeln gekriegt und musste das Gesicht wieder auf diesen ekelhaften Boden sinken lassen.

Deirdre Bunson

Sie haben Sam in beide Knie geschossen. Man hörte die Schüsse, dann hörte man Sam schreien. Ein paar Lehrer riefen etwas, aber da fielen gleich wieder Schüsse, und wieder schwirrten überall die Querschläger herum, und noch mehr Lampen gingen zu Bruch. Gary und Brendan brüllten die Lehrer an, sie sollten den Mund halten. Die wollten nicht bloß die Sportler töten. Die wollten alle in diesem Raum töten.

Dustin Williams

Ich habe ungefähr einen Meter neben Deirdre gelegen. Sie ist durchgedreht, als sie Sam in die Knie geschossen haben. Ich glaube wirklich, dass sie nicht mehr an sich selbst gedacht hat. Sie hat Brendan angebrüllt: »Du Loser, du mieses Schwein.« Sie hat gesagt, er soll das Gewehr weg-

legen. »Dann sehen wir ja, wie stark du wirklich bist«, hat sie geschrien.
Alle verrenken die Köpfe, um was zu sehen. Brendan macht einen Schritt auf sie zu. Deirdre sagt nichts mehr. Er kniet sich neben sie und drückt ihr das Gewehr an die Wange. Sie schreit auf und zuckt zurück. Wahrscheinlich war der Lauf noch heiß und hat ihr das Gesicht verbrannt.
Ich weiß noch, was er gesagt hat: »He, Cheerleader, was glaubst du, wie egal mir das ist, ob du mich für einen Loser hältst oder nicht? Ich weiß selbst, dass ich einer bin. Und willst du wissen, woher ich das weiß? Weil du und deine !*&$Freunde mich, seit ich hier bin, jeden Tag daran erinnert haben.«
Dann drückt er ihr den Lauf in den Nacken. Richtig sadistisch. Deirdre wimmert und fleht ihn an, dass er sie nicht erschießen soll. Jetzt kommt Gary dazu und sagt irgendwas von einem Unfall, den Deirdre gehabt hätte. Die beiden lachen. Ein Lehrer – ich glaube, Mr Flanagan – schreit sie an, und sie schießen in den Fußboden. Ich habe an der Wange gespürt, wie der Boden gebebt hat.
Brendan flucht und sagt, er habe daneben geschossen. Gary erklärt, er mag ja daneben geschossen haben, aber immerhin sei jetzt ein schönes Loch im Holzboden.

Paul Burns

Nach der Autopsie schrieben die Zeitungen, die beiden hätten keine Drogen genommen, aber wenn Sie mich fragen, haben die sich aufgeführt wie völlig zugekiffte Irre. Wie sie da lachend herumgelaufen sind und in den Boden geschossen haben, dass das Holz nur so krachte und splitterte. Ich konnte nur noch beten, dass ihnen irgendwann die Munition ausgeht.

Dustin Williams

Das war unheimlich, als sie dann in den Boden geschossen haben. Als ob sie jetzt total ausgerastet wären. Plötzlich klingelte mein Handy und da haben sie aufgehört. Meine Mutter hatte mir das Handy für den Ball mitgegeben, und ich hatte es Dustin zum Aufbewahren gegeben. Brendan ging rüber und nahm es Dustin aus der Tasche.
Man hat Ihnen doch erzählt, was er gesagt hat, oder? Meine Mutter hat gefragt, ob ich da sei, und Brendan hat gesagt, ja, aber ich könne jetzt nicht mit ihr sprechen. Und als meine Mutter gefragt hat, ob ich sie zurückrufen könnte, hat er gesagt, wohl kaum, weil ich dann wahrscheinlich schon tot wäre.

Chelsea Baker

Das war echt krank. Wie die den Leuten an die Köpfe gestoßen haben. Und dann die Sache mit dem Handy und mit der Mutter von Chelsea Baker … Weiß auch nicht, aber das alles war total krank.

Paul Burns

Sam lag auf dem Boden und schluchzte und stöhnte, das war ganz furchtbar. Jemand schrie, wenn man nicht sofort Hilfe holen würde, könnte er verbluten. Und einer der beiden sagte daraufhin bloß: »Ach ja, tatsächlich?« Genau das wollten sie nämlich. Er sollte einen langsamen, schrecklichen Tod sterben.

Deirdre Bunson

Ich hörte so ein metallisches Klicken. Erst wusste ich nicht, was das war. Ich konnte mich nicht weit genug umdrehen, um was zu sehen. Aber dann begriff ich, dass Brendan und Gary ihre Gewehre nachluden.

Beth Bender

Als ich hörte, wie sie nachluden, sah ich zu Beth rüber. In ihrem Blick war nur noch Verzweiflung. Denn plötzlich war uns beiden klar: Brendan und Gary waren richtig gut bewaffnet. Sie waren auf alles vorbereitet. Denen würde nicht so bald die Munition ausgehen.

Dick Flanagan